What the Bible Means to Me

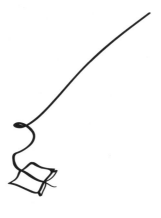

Testimonies of how God's Word impacts lives

Edited by
Catherine Mackenzie

CHRISTIAN
FOCUS

Contents

Alec Motyer

Retired principal of Trinity College, Bristol, England, Alec has been both a pastor and a professor during a life spent serving the Church. Throughout his professional career he has become well known for his work on the Old Testament and the book of Isaiah in particular.

I have loved the Bible as far back as I can remember. For this, thanks is due to what is ordinarily called a 'chance'. My parents left me as a baby in my grandmother's care for a weekend, and the weekend stretched out to become my first seven years. During that time a very ordinary old lady lovingly shared her extensive Bible knowledge and the love which she felt for Bible stories and Bible truth. Others may see 'chance'. I see the deliberate plan of the God of all grace. Did Grandma enter into discussion of whether the Bible is true? In what sense it is the Word of God? What does 'inspired' mean? No. Such topics never entered her head, but, all-unknowingly, the way she shared even the simplest Bible story imparted unthought-out, implicit convictions that here indeed is truth; this is indeed God's Word.

Nothing has shaken these certainties. In the face of liberal theological education, and the often hostile criticism of the Bible by teachers, nothing could persuade me to accept anything that cast doubt on Scripture or diminished its glory, and speciality. When I did not know the answer to arguments,

I put them 'on the long finger'. Confident that the Bible would yet vindicate itself against all comers. And the same is still true: problems still arise, and are there to be wrestled with, and some must remain awaiting answers. But problems are not doubts. Years of reading, thinking, and learning have turned childish intuition into mature certainty. 'Here' (as the Queen's Coronation Service asserted) 'is Wisdom; this is the Royal Law; these are the lively Oracles of God.'

The Bible is still to me the lovely and beloved book. That in itself is sufficient to get me out of bed in the morning! For it is the book of the knowledge of God, and the repository of eternal and saving truth. First, I find that the Bible is the life-changing Book by virtue of its own inherent spiritual power. I know well that when Psalm 119:105 says, 'Your Word is a lamp' it is thinking of the hand-held torch to show where next to put our feet, and the car head-lamp illuminating the road ahead. But it is also an infra-red lamp – a health or heat lamp. We read our Bibles and over the years we find that we are being ministered to, nourished, at the secret roots of our being. It's never true that 'we get nothing' out of our Bible reading. Last week's food nourished us even though we now have no memory of the menu! The living God imparts himself to us in his holy Word.

Secondly, at the conscious level, the Bible in its every part is profitable for doctrine, reproof, correction and instruction – respectively, to teach us the truth, to correct errors in mind and life, to order our conduct in true directions, and to educate us in righteousness. It is God's school and university course from infancy to graduation (2 Tim. 3:14–17). Blessed are those who, like Timothy and me, were given a start in infancy by godly grandmothers.

Thirdly – and above all – without the Bible we would not know Jesus in whom are stored all the treasures of God's wisdom and knowledge. With four Gospels compared with one of everything else, the very construction of the Bible is a divine signal that this one thing is four times as important as anything else: read the Gospels, follow the example of Mary who 'took her seat at Jesus' feet, and went on hearing his word' (Luke 10:39). What she did once we can do everyday – that's what the Bible means to me.

For Your Information:

CHRIST'S DIVINITY AND HUMANITY

Bible passages which speak of Jesus Christ as God –
John 1:1, John 20:28, Romans 9:5, Philippians 2:11,
and Colossians 1:16.

Bible passages which speak of Jesus Christ's humanity –
Luke 2:7, Luke 2:40, Luke 8:23, John 1:14, John 4:6
and Hebrews 4:15.

Ann Johnston

Ann is the U.K. Co-ordinator of the Geared for Growth Bible Studies published by W.E.C. and Christian Focus Publications. Ann loves nothing more than a walk around the beautiful grounds of Mount Stewart on the Ards Peninsula, Northern Ireland, followed by a wee cup of tea.

I love Bible Study. I love delving into God's Word and discovering new things. Things I'd never understood before. Things I'd never seen, and there they are revealed to me by God in his own personal way. Things for Ann's eyes only. Things that are very poignant to my circumstances at that point in time and beyond. That's who he is, so personal, so knowledgeable, so wise and so loving. He is the supreme authority over all that exists and yet he sees me, Ann Johnston, a nobody! The world has never heard of me, my name is not emblazoned in lights somewhere or on the tip of everyone's tongue. Yet he, the Supreme One, the one with all the power and authority, he sees me, he knows me, he communicates with me. When he speaks to me he says, 'Ann'. I am known!

And in response I long to know Him, I long to know what his thoughts are, how he sees things, what's on his mind, what pleases Him. As I open my Bible each day this is what I long for, Him. What new thing will I discover, what new thought will he communicate with my heart today, and what change will this encounter bring about in my life, in my thought patterns, on the way I view situations, on the actions that I will then take and the consequences that will then ensue. I so want to take the path that leads to Life! As a child of Light living in the Kingdom of Darkness, (right slap bang in the middle of enemy territory). I want to discover God's path through this barren and desolate land. I not only want to, I need to, because I have tasted of this Life and its taste cannot be forgotten. There is no substitute.

And so I come to Him, my Heavenly Father, each day as I open the pages of his book, wanting fresh manna, wanting more, just simply wanting.

Allan MacDonald

Allan is a graduate of Edinburgh College of Art and has since returned to the Highlands of Scotland to dedicate most of his time to painting this extraordinary corner of God's World.

It's sometimes helpful to look at the Bible through objective eyes, as though momentarily detached from its personal significance. Does it really reveal the voice, mind and heart of a great Supernatural Being? Or does it sound like a collection of ancient myths and truths – wise, but nevertheless utterly human? How can you tell the difference?

For it to be the former, it must be simple yet at the same time fathomless. Simple, for all men must be able to understand it, to avoid charges of elitism or exclusivity. And profound, because any communication claiming to unveil the supernatural (God) while concurrently grappling with the natural world (us) must of necessity be complex.

The Bible fulfils this criteria. What can be simpler than Paul the apostle's reply to his jailer in Philippi, who asked him what he must do to be saved. 'Believe in the Lord Jesus Christ and you will be saved,' or Jesus' own words, 'I am the Way, the Truth and the Life'.

For complexity, think of the ways the shadows of the Old Testament become reality in the New Testament. One example is the Passover lamb, described in the Old Testament. If the blood of that lamb was over your doorway, you were safe. This is mirrored in the New Testament, where another sacrifice is recorded and becomes the central tenet of the Christian faith... the 'safeness' of trusting in Christ's blood, shed on Calvary.

Could such an extraordinary concept have been conceived and sustained by a wide variety of authors, over hundreds of years?

Every great book has a hero, and the Bible is no different in this regard, and it is in this that I see another clear sign of the supernatural origins of Scripture.

Remembering when it was written, in an age where power depended on brutal, military strength, it is bewildering that the hero of the book should be portrayed chiefly as a servant. It is impossible for me to believe that Isaiah 53 is a text of solely human construction. Even today, true servant-hood and grace are still radical, alternative behaviour traits, absurdly difficult for any man or woman to have or sustain. It's hard to imagine the impact of these words when they were written; '...his form was marred beyond human likeness ... he had no beauty or majesty to attract us to him ... he was despised and rejected of men ... he poured out his life unto death, and was numbered with the transgressors ...'. Society today adores ambition, exalts the shocking, praises the cutting edge, extols self-esteem ... but meekness? Leadership through submission?

There's plenty of pride in the Bible, of course. Many of the leading figures, from Abraham, Jacob and David through to the disciples, have bucket-fulls of the stuff. In this sense, the Bible is self-evidently not propaganda. It doesn't hide the flaws, the unaccountable weaknesses of some of its main characters. Out of their volatile lives emerges another story that runs alongside them. The hero, the Leader, the Saviour, the supernatural being who was present at the creation of the world, suggests another way, one beyond not only our imagination, but our ability to fabricate or emulate.

One final thought. Very few suggest that Jesus, whose claim in Scripture is to be the 'Son of God', was a lunatic. Yet everyone else since, who has made that claim, has been at best deluded, at worst psychotic and has been exposed as such immediately. This implies to me that there was complete harmony between his claims and his life, as witnessed by those around him. This is a testimony not to be taken lightly.

So it is, that as we view the Bible objectively, its truth and honesty break through into our subjectivity, and force us to consider a staggering reality ... that it really has supernatural authorship. Science fiction has never been more popular, thriving on our longing to communicate with other life forms, to comfort ourselves that we're not alone. Yet all the time, lying on our shelves, is the ultimate communiqué from another realm.

Caroline Cox

Caroline is a cross-bench member of the British House of Lords. She also is the founder and CEO of an organisation called the Humanitarian Aid Relief Trust (HART). She has campaigned for humanitarian causes, particularly relating to disability.

I believe the Bible is ultimately precious as the record of ways in which God has revealed himself over the centuries as the God of Love – and it is this which makes our faith unique.

The Old Testament records God's care for his people and his response to human failings: at times frightening and challenging, but also reassuring in the promises of forgiveness and blessing for those who turn to him in repentance and obedience. And there are books such as the Psalms – timeless treasures of prayer and praise.

The New Testament brings the glorious news of Incarnation when God manifests his love in his willingness to accept the limitations, challenges and suffering inherent in human life. The New Testament also brings a new and overriding commandment: 'A new command I give you: Love one another. As I have loved you, so you must love one another.'(John 13:34). The book of Acts is a gripping story of the ways in which the Apostles responded to our Lord's command and the epistles are as meaningful today as when they were first written.

Love is inevitably costly, as demonstrated in the many trials and tribulations experienced by Jesus and his ultimate sacrifice of an agonising death on the cross. Christianity is not a 'comfortable' religion in terms of this world's comforts – as the 250 million Christians suffering persecution today can testify. But they also testify to the fulfilment of God's promise to 'be a very present help in trouble'; to the reality of that 'peace which passes all understanding' and to the power of indestructible love. Whenever I have the privilege of being with brothers and sisters suffering persecution, I am humbled and inspired by their living faith and radiant joy in the Good News of the Bible.

As Christians, we are uniquely blessed to have a faith rooted in the Word of God recorded in the Bible and revealed in the Word Incarnate. If anyone asks me what my God is like, all I need to do is to refer to the Bible as his revelation of himself in word and in his person.

I will never forget one of the great challenges to my faith. I had been visiting the peoples suffering in war-torn southern Sudan during the war waged against them by the Islamist regime in Khartoum – a war in which two million died and four million were displaced. I had been walking through the killing fields of Bahr-El-Ghazal, in the aftermath of a massacre perpetrated by Government of Sudan soldiers and the mujahedin who fought alongside them. After walking fifteen kilometres through human corpses, slaughtered cattle and burnt homes, I sat by my tent 'there were no houses left standing' and wept. All the familiar challenges to faith assailed me: how does a God of Love, who is omniscient and omnipotent, allow such suffering to be inflicted on innocent women and children?

Then my thoughts turned to the Bible and it occurred to me that one reason why we in 'comfortable Christianity' may not be able to come to terms with the reality of evil is reflected in the way in which we celebrate Christmas. Of course it is right to rejoice in Love Incarnate – a God who loves us so much that he is prepared to become a frail human baby, sharing all the vulnerability of humanity. But while we continue to enjoy the festive season with Christmas parties, presents and all the happy paraphernalia of our traditional celebrations, we often forget that, while Mary was rejoicing in the birth of Jesus, countless other mothers were weeping for the slaughter of their sons by Herod. While we continue to ignore this part of the reality of the original Christmas, it is not surprising if our contemporary theology finds it hard to cope with the continuation of man-made suffering in our day. My thoughts then turned to the end of Jesus' life, the suffering and anguish of death by crucifixion. All that his mother Mary could do was to stand at the foot of the Cross and be with her Son in profound grief. Finally, it occurred to me that part of a Christian's calling may be to be prepared to attend whatever Calvaries our Lord may call us to attend – and to be present, as Mary was, in grief, love and profound respect.

In the Bible, we find the whole gamut of human experience and the manifestation of God's love throughout. That is why I cherish the Bible: there is no other faith which can celebrate a God of Love who loves us so much that he entered into the frailty and frustration of human experience, its challenges, joys and heartache, revealing himself as Love Incarnate. And every part of the Bible reflects this amazing, almost unbelievable, revelation of the God Who made the Universe, Who is also God Emmanuel – God with us and in us, in love and amazing grace.

For Your Information

The New Testament

The New Testament has in it: four Gospels; the book of Acts; twenty-one Epistles; and the book of Revelation.

<u>Four Gospels</u>
Matthew
Mark
Luke
John

<u>Twenty-one Epistles</u>
Romans
1 Corinthians
2 Corinthians
Galatians
Ephesians
Philippians
Colossians
1 Thessalonians
2 Thessalonians
1 Timothy
2 Timothy
Titus
Philemon
Hebrews
James
1 Peter
2 Peter
1 John
2 John
3 John
Jude

Bob Bond

As an illustrator and comic-strip artist Bob has worked on several projects including a children's book by D.L. Moody, the nineteenth-century evangelist called *When President Lincoln Listened.*

As a comic-strip artist, I have always loved a good yarn with a surprising or unexpected ending. My mother told me some great stories as she bounced me on her knee as a child. She loved her Bible, so not surprisingly my bed-time tales were of floating arks, falling walls, and fishermen leaving their nets to follow Jesus. Early in life she taught me the Lord's Prayer and The Twenty-third Psalm, and she would quote scripture liberally at appropriate moments. And sometimes inappropriate!

Jesus, of course, was the story-teller supreme. Often his stories had unexpected endings. He told how a young man came to his dad one day and said, 'Give me what's mine and I'll be off ...' And his dad did just that – surprise number one! And later on, when the silly lad had lost everything, he decided to go home and ask dad if he could be one of his servants. Here comes surprise number two! Dad saw him coming, ran to meet him, threw his arms around him, kissed him, gave him presents, and announced a party!

Older brother was not in a party mood. No surprise there... 'Listen,' said dad, 'the party is for ME, not your kid brother, because I thought he was dead and he's not!'

'And' said Jesus 'your Heavenly Father is like that. He doesn't sit there with a big stick, waiting to beat you up. When someone finds their way back to God, they have a party in Heaven.' That's the final happy-ending frame of the picture-strip.

If there is a God – and I believe with all my heart that there is – then I need to know what he is like. The Bible, and the words of Jesus, help me to understand the nature of God, and what he requires of me... 'To act justly and to love mercy and to walk humbly with my God' (Micah 6:8).

The Bible is my final arbiter in matters of belief and action. As my mother told me, 'Read it in, pray it down, and work it out.' I'm still trying to do that, with Christ's help, seventy years later.

Like many of you who are reading this, I've had to contend with tragedy on my Christian journey – three years ago I lost my darling wife to cancer. I can't explain this. Yet even at those times when God doesn't make sense, we hold on to his Word, his promises, and his presence.

For Your Information

The word Bible comes from a Greek word Biblia which means 'books'.

Brian Cosby

Brian is an ordained minister in the Presbyterian Church in America. He has written several books including *John Bunyan: The Journey of a Pilgrim* in the Trailblazers series and continues to write articles for various magazines and journals.

I love fly-fishing. I remember casting my line from the middle of the Firehole River in Yellowstone National Park in Wyoming on a beautiful August day – as I took in the full array of God's creative handiwork. The bright purple and red flowers provided a perfect contrast to the river gorge as it ran beneath a brilliant blue sky. Along the banks of the river stood a variety of indigenous trees, all of which stood strong, healthy and full of life. I felt the same.

Meditating upon the Word of God is a means by which he ushers us unto the pastures, waters, and banks of his transformative grace. Psalm 1:3 tells us that we are "blessed" when we delight in God's Word and meditate upon it day and night. The Psalmist writes that the one who does this "is like a tree planted by streams of water that yields its fruit in its season, and its leaf does not wither".

Like Jacob wrestling with the angel (Gen. 32), I need to wrestle, study, meditate, and chew on God's Word until I find myself 'blessed' and bearing fruit. When the winds of cultural pressure or temptations of doubt blow against my frail faith,

I need to be planted – with deep roots in the promises of God's Word.

But it doesn't stop there. All of Scripture points to the Savior of sinners, Jesus Christ. He is my Living Water (John 4:10) and Bread of Life (John 6:35). As the Word of God (John 1:1), Jesus reminds me that it is only through faith alone in his substitutionary death and perfect obedience that I may enter boldly before God's throne of grace and take delight in the truth of God's Word, the Bible. The Bible means more than a mere unfolding of divine revelation; it is the stream of water to my tree of faith, planted for God's glory and my joy.

For Your Information:

The Bible was written over a 1,500 year span (from 1400 B.C. to A.D. 100). It took over forty generations for it to be completed. It was written by over forty authors from many walks of life (e.g. – kings, peasants, philosophers, fishermen, poets, statesmen, scholars). The Bible was also written in different places (e.g. – wilderness, dungeons, palaces) and at different times (e.g. – war, peace).It was written on three continents (Asia, Africa, and Europe) and in three languages (Hebrew, Aramaic, and Greek).

Cathie Aberdour

Cathie is a member of Wycliffe Bible Translators and has translated the New Testament and parts of the Old into the language of the Apurinã people of the Amazon.

Recently I held up my Bible in front of the Primary Seven class. 'This book has changed my life,' I said. I then asked them what this book was. I was stunned when no one knew. Then a child asked if it was a dictionary!

When I was in my early twenties I began to realise in a fresh way that the Bible was no ordinary book but truly God's Word, the answer to all life's problems and that it gave the way of eternal salvation.

I was challenged by the fact that in Scotland you can get your own copy by a simple visit to a bookstore, but throughout the world many people have no access to God's written Word.

A young couple came to my church who were on their way to Papua New Guinea to translate the New Testament into the language of a Bibleless people group there. This challenged me greatly and so I went to Bible school to study this book in greater detail, then I went with the Wycliffe Bible Translators to Brazil to translate God's Word into the Apurinã language.

It has been a great joy to see that the Bible has not only changed my life but is changing Apurinã lives. Chico is one of the Apurinã who has helped me to translate God's Word into his language. I remember the day we were translating the opening chapters of Genesis. Chico told me of when he was a boy. His grannie had asked him to go down to the stream to fetch water. As he was lazily filling the bucket he noticed the sun's reflection on the water. Then he said to himself, 'I wonder who made the sun?' Then he thought further. 'I wonder who made the world and who made people?' He returned to his grannie and asked her. 'I don't know,' was her honest reply. At that point in the story Chico's face beamed as he pointed to God's Word and said, 'Now I know'.

How does God's Word change lives? It's because it's true from Genesis 1:1 to Revelation 22:21. When translating Matthew 12:24 where the Pharisees said that Jesus was casting out demons by Beelzebub's power, Chico didn't want me to translate it like that. 'But that's not true about Jesus,' he said. 'But it's what the Pharisees said about Jesus,' I told him. One evidence of the truth of God's Word is that nothing is covered up. Jesus says in John 8:31,32 'If you continue in my Word, then are you my disciples indeed. And you shall know the truth, and the truth shall make you free.' (KJV)) It's only God's Word that can set us free from the power of sin and enable us to live lives that are pleasing to ourselves and more importantly to God.

Chris Woodman

As the Minister of The Lighthouse Church, Forres, Chris ministers to a community that has long had connections to the R.A.F. in the North East of Scotland.

What can I say of such a treasure? The Bible is nothing less than the Word that God my Father speaks to me; the Word concerning God the Son given for me; the Word ministered by God the Holy Spirit to me.

The Bible is my inexhaustible source of truth in a world of lies; my inextinguishable light in a world of darkness; my sure, inerrant and infallible guide in a world that is lost. Yet I find that it is a battleground for my soul.

My old self, the flesh, loathes this Word, whilst my new self, born of the Spirit of God, delights in it and thrives upon it. The Word is a bitter taste to my flesh, starving it, stifling it, strangling it, tearing it down, exposing it and condemning it. For the new life in me, the Word is the sweetest of tastes, the most nourishing and choicest of foods, the most invigorating breath of life; ever building me up, affirming, encouraging, edifying.

Above all else the Bible is most precious to me for it draws my eyes, my thoughts, my aspirations, my ambitions, my longings and my heart away from myself and sets it firmly upon he who is so worthy – Jesus Christ my Saviour and my Lord who, along with the Father and the Spirit, is to be forever praised!

For Your Information

National Bible Societies exist because millions lack the Bible in a language they can understand or at a price they can afford. At the same time millions still have no understanding of the Bible's value. Bible Societies refer to this as Bible poverty.

Here is their vision:

They are working to see a day when the Bible's God-given revelation, inspiration and wisdom is shaping the lives and communities of people everywhere.

The task is huge as well as urgent. More than 4,400 languages still wait for even one book of the Bible.

Though a billion people can't read, only three per cent of languages have the Bible in audio.

Every five seconds, someone goes blind but the complete Braille Bible exists in only thirty-five languages.

There is Bible Poverty even in countries that have been traditionally referred to as Christian as the Bible is no longer central to everyday life.

Christine Farenhorst

As a wife, mother and author based in Ontario, Canada, Christine's experience of the Bible is that it is a book that must be read for meaningful and happy living. That is why she has entitled this chapter – 'O Taste and See!'

Many years ago, when I was a young girl and just married, I worked at the University of Guelph in the Department of Political Studies. My secretarial duties often required that I serve as a messenger between our department and various other departments. Consequently, I met an older woman down the hall who was secretary to a professor of surveying, or of something of that sort.

Bernice, a friendly, short, stoop-shouldered woman, with eyes that protruded abnormally from a small olive face, was Jewish. Talking was her second nature. Proudly keeping me up-to-date with son number one who was a doctor and son number two who was a lawyer, she also frequently mentioned that she and her husband had paid for every penny of their education. Describing in glorious detail, during the course of the time that I was acquainted with her, clothes she bought, furniture she chose, and the interior of the car she drove, she regularly gave me hints for bargain shopping.

It was obvious that Bernice was not overly fond of her husband, often implying that her spouse did not earn enough money to suit her and that it was a good thing she herself worked hard. The woman never stood still, was always on the move, and totally avoided serious conversation. It seemed almost as if she was playing hide-and-seek with the inevitable; as if she was running away from the last enemy of all those living; and ignoring the one who patiently stalks all mankind – death. Bernice wanted to hear nothing of the God of the Bible, shrugging indifferently at my, usually inept, attempts to tell her where my affections lay.

Several years later, I traveled from our home in northern Ontario to visit my parents in Hamilton. Snugly ensconced in the soft seats of a Greyhound bus with my two and three-year-old daughters, I was immensely surprised when a small woman stopped next to me in the bus aisle during our stop-over in Guelph.

"Bernice," I exclaimed. "How nice to see you!"

She blinked nervously, smiled at the girls and wiped her fogged-up glasses. The girls said "hi", looking at her curiously. It was a dark, dreary day. And such was Bernice's face – dark and dreary.

"Please sit next to us, Bernice."

I took one of the girls on my lap and she squeezed in next to us, politely inquiring, as the bus began its journey onward, about my husband, our home and the children. But it was evident that she was distracted.

"How is your husband, Bernice?"

"He died."

"I'm very sorry to hear it."

She shrugged, her well-made, elegant raincoat encasing her in a grey cocoon. Then she began to talk – and there was no stopping her. Her sons were both well-established around the Toronto, Ontario, area. However, neither son wanted her to live with them. As a matter of fact, they had made it perfectly clear that even her visits were not appreciated. She was retired now, and her days were long, empty. There was, as she put it, nothing left – nothing at all.

When she was finished, I spoke, albeit haltingly, of her need for a friend, an eternal Friend, a Savior. And, unable to walk away, she listened. Recounting times that I also had felt lost and abandoned, I suggested that she obtain a Bible and read about the Savior who was always there. She smiled and told me I was nice to care about her but she was old, too old to change.

"You are welcome to visit us," I responded and gave her our address.

At the Hamilton station, she stumbled out of the bus ahead of us and I never saw her again.

"O taste and see that the LORD is good! Happy is the man who takes refuge in him!" (Ps. 34:8 ESV)

For Your Information

The Old Testament was written in Hebrew and the New Testament was written in Greek but now the Bible is written in 6,000 different languages around the world!

Clark Walls

Clark used to be a taxi driver but is now a bus driver in Inverness, the capital of the Highlands of Scotland.

I was brought up in Foyers by the shores of Loch Ness and lived next door to the local bus driver. My aunty still reminds me that I used to tell everyone that when I grew up I was going to be a bus driver and I even dressed up in a bus driver's uniform. However, my mother had her sights set higher for me. She hoped that I would become a Christian so she took me to Sunday School and then later we went to church. In those early years a seed was planted in my heart by hearing the Word of God, the Bible.

When I left home I gradually stopped going to church but years later a friend persuaded me to go to church again, so I went and heard the Bible being read and explained. It sounded so different to what I had heard before. It seemed that the seed which was planted years ago had received the water it needed and I realised that things were not alright between God and me. I realised that a prayer now and again was not enough but that I needed this living Word (the Bible) to explain that 'Anyone who calls on the name of the Lord will be saved' (Rom. 10:13 KJV). That is why the Bible is the most important book that I will ever read. It shows me how to live and how to have eternal life. It is many books within a book. There are stories of love and stories of beginnings. There are stories of wars and stories of victories. Stories of sadness and of joy. You will find advice on marriage, relationships and parenting. You will find help in loneliness, fear, friendship, worry and dozens of other subjects.

Although the King James Version of the Bible is 400 years old, the book of Genesis was written many hundred years before that and yet it is as current and up-to-date as today's newspaper. There are so many different needs that we have. And if we search the scriptures God will reveal himself to us in remarkable ways. I find it so comforting to know that whatever situation I find myself in, whether it's a problem or something I want to be joyful about, God is always there to hear my prayers.

My uncle passed away last year and a friend who knew him well used to call him 'the oracle' as he was so informative in so many subjects. Shortly after his passing I heard someone say, 'when an old man dies a library burns down'. I understand what they meant. But God's Word, the Bible is the living Word so it never dies.

This is what God says: 'So shall my Word be that goeth forth out of my mouth: it shall not return unto me void, but it shall accomplish that which I please, and it shall prosper in the thing whereto I sent it' (Isa. 55:11 KJV).

My childhood dream of becoming a bus driver came true but better still my mother lived to see her dream come true when I became a Christian.

For Your Information

Abraham was the first person in the Bible to be called a Hebrew. The oldest person in the Bible was Methuselah. He died at the age of 969 years old.

Two men in the Bible never died! Their names were Enoch and Elijah and God took them to heaven.

Colin Buchanan

A seven-times Golden Guitar winner, Colin is also an APRA and ARIA award winner. A regular on Australian national T.V. and radio for over fifteen years and a leading children's entertainer, Colin Buchanan is a hard man to pin down!

At school I enjoyed subjects with stories. You'd think that would give literature the edge, but no, it was ancient history that really grabbed me. Mrs. Elstub delivered The Peloponnesian Wars with all the vigour of an angry Spartan. The stories came alive.

I liked subjects you could see. For me, maths was the absolute antithesis of this. Sure, times tables were useful when sharing sweets and counting has proven to be one of the enduringly useful skills of my entire education but quadratic equations and trigonometry ... Haven't seen any of that stuff in the wild.

Geography, was different. River valleys, erosion, vegetation, urban settlement, infrastructure, commercial precincts – everywhere I looked, there was geography.

Apart from proving to you that I'm certainly no brainiac, what I've told you about my schooling gives away a few secrets about me. I tend to do the best at the things I enjoy. And I certainly enjoy a good story.

One of my earliest memories of the Bible was as a pre-school boy sitting in church in Dublin, thumbing through my little New Testament. The Good Samaritan picture was my favourite – the beaten man being helped tenderly onto the Samaritan's donkey. You could say my love of the Bible is just because I am a child of church-going parents. But the reason I told you about my favourite subjects at school is because the Bible is so much more to me than a nostalgic memory of my upbringing.

I love the stories of the Bible. Those simple, powerful parables of Jesus captured my childish imagination. Here was a storytelling King who called the little children to come. He was himself part of the amazing Christmas story, his incarnation. The events of his life were so rooted in the real world, with real people. And his brutal death was so tragic and noble and graphic. Then the crescendo of his resurrection and the beginning of a new story, the story of the church.

Not only did I love the stories of the Bible, but I felt from a very early age that they were part of a much larger story. I knew that I was called to become part of this story by faith. It was as if the living, risen Jesus didn't simple say, 'follow me,' but 'follow me, Colin.' The story of forgiveness in Christ, of everlasting life through him, of a redeemed life lived with and for him is still the most compelling story I have ever heard. I have staked my life on it.

I love the Bible because its truth is a truth you can see. Jesus walked in the bumps-and-lumps, flesh-and-bone, water-and-wine, life-and-death world we live in. Sure, I've come to appreciate the organisation of Bible truths, numbered and tagged to help me appreciate more of the nature of God, what happened on the cross, what the church is and lots of other things. But it's the realness of it all that is compelling. There is so much learning and teaching in the Christian life and yet all of life becomes the classroom.

The eternal sufficiency of God has everything to do with, say, life in the supermarket aisle. Drop a tin in the trolley. I'm enjoying the gracious bounty of temporal provision from the hand of the completely non-contingent God. He needs no feeding. I'm in the line, getting out my wallet. He pays for nothing. Savings or credit? My account is filled to overflowing with the righteousness of Christ. Enter your PIN. I am eternally, un-hackably secure, encrypted by the seal of God's own Holy Spirit. 'Have a nice day.' 'I know the plans I have for you ...' I head into the remains of the day held in God's everlasting arms... I see the Bible in life. God's truth is real.

I love the fact that the Bible is hands-on. No room for sofa slobs sitting back with crisps and a drink watching the big game and indignantly spewing out their 'expert' opinion about how their team should have played. I'm ever in the field of play, getting down and dirty in the game. If the Bible isn't hands-on, perhaps truth isn't getting through.

I know I can be like the fuel tanker that runs out of diesel. 20,000 gallons in the trailer, unused as my engine gasps and stops, dying of thirst because, for all its high-octane potential, it never made its way into my tank and my motor. So close and yet so far. Truth in the head but not in the life is perilous. I praise God for compelling, insightful authors and preachers who, by God's grace, bring the truth to bear on my life, who take the grand and lofty truths and fire them like harpoons, penetrating my everyday.

There is so, so much to know from the Scriptures. I love the challenge of being truly hands-on with the Bible. I love how a simple truth embraced, believed and lived can be such a powerful dynamic as I see it explode in godly, simple obedience – in a child, in a parent, in an old person – maybe even in my own life. God begins a good work and he carries it on to the day of completion. As I get hands-on with the Bible I discover the priceless privilege that the Almighty God gets hands-on with me.

It occurred to me the other day that, for the believer, the Bible will pass. It sounds like a dangerous statement to the careful evangelical. But imagine if you were given this choice: to have a lover's letter or to spend the rest of your life in the very presence of your lover. The Word is treasure because it comes from the very mouth of the Living God. And one day the time for paper will be past. I will not only meet the author, not only hear his voice, but I will join with the overjoyed redeemed of every time and tribe and tongue, seeing and worshipping the Word made flesh, our Jesus, enthroned and exalted at the right hand of the Father.

Douglas Kelly

Douglas is the Richard Jordan Professor of Theology at Reformed Theological Seminary, Charlotte, North Carolina. He is married to Caroline and is father to five adult children.

The Holy Bible is so inter-twined with every aspect of my childhood that I could not separate it from them, even if I tried. Every room of the main family home was filled with an atmosphere of quiet and generally happy belief in the Lord who spoke to us in his written Word: table blessings at every meal, evening family prayers, calm Sabbaths of worship at church and a pervading sense of family and neighborly love and fellowship between services, visits of relatives who so often mentioned some text of Scripture in their regular conversation about things that were happening. As far as I remember, all of the long-time family servants believed in Christ, and not infrequently quoted portions of Scripture. I well remember quotations from my much loved, elderly nannie (who died at a considerable age, when I was eight; I think she had been born only nine or ten years after the bad institution of slavery ended). I can still see myself seated on her lap, with her Bible open. She had not been advantaged with enough education to write, but at least could read a certain amount: especially, God's Word. What I particularly recall was her love for Jesus.

I still remember how she told me about the betrayal of Jesus, and how he died on the cross for our sins, and rose again to get us into heaven, and that he was with us in the room that day.

When I was at the wake for my grandmother at age nine, with a large rural home filled with people, overflowing onto the surround porches, I can still visualize an elderly cousin sitting down beside my rocking chair in the intense July heat (long before air-conditioning), and holding up an old-fashioned funeral home fan, with Holman-Hunt's picture of Christ standing outside the door, bearing the words of Revelation 3:20 underneath the picture. She then asked me if I had opened my heart's door to the risen Lord? I told this good woman that I did not know when it had happened, but that he had filled my soul as long as I could remember, and that I looked forward to seeing my grandmother, and our Saviour himself, one happy day.

In later years, in my early teens, I used to work in the fields with one of our tenants (on the old family plantation in North Carolina, where I lived with elderly relatives each summer). He was a bright, deeply committed Christian, a father and grandfather, who radiated the Lord's presence as we worked our way down the rows of the cotton and tobacco fields in ninety degrees Fahrenheit heat and thick humidity. I recall his frequent speaking of the cleansing power of the blood of Christ (from I John 1), and of the joy of a life yielded to the Holy Spirit. He (as had my nannie, long before) definitely believed that the Lord was calling me into the ministry. During those hot summers, my great-aunt usually came into my bedroom every night to lead in prayer. Before she prayed, she often talked to me about what prayer meant; how it brings us into the divine throne-room (sometimes referring to Hebrews 7), and what it means to pray in Jesus' name, and how – although we should be specific in our requests – our underlying attitude must always be that of Christ in the Garden: "Thy will be done." Then, she at times quoted the Gospel verse: "He hath done all things well!"

Through the many decades I have lived since a spiritually privileged childhood and youth, I have felt very humbled to have experienced such divine goodness through an ever-present

Word in the lives of those I loved the most, and indeed – in the general demeanour of the entire community of which I was a small part. Such divine goodness made me – and still makes me – say with Isaiah: "LORD, here am I, send me".

Dale Ralph Davis

Ralph lives in rural Tennessee with his wife. Prior to that he was pastor of Woodland Presbyterian Church, Hattiesburg, Mississippi and Professor of Old Testament at Reformed Theological Seminary, Jackson, Mississippi.

Remember when we were eating barbecued bear meat in Colorado? There are moments in one's life that one just doesn't forget. Perhaps they didn't seem so momentous at the time – and yet they stick in one's mind. And now as I look back I can recognize certain 'moments' that have shaped how I regard the Scriptures.

The first moment is a rather long one – my father's preaching ministry. He was a United Presbyterian pastor, and in that calling he gave premier attention to his preaching ministry. I can remember some bits of sermons and handling of texts. But particulars matter little – what is so clear now was his focus. Whether morning sermon or evening sermon, his preaching was consistently an explanation of a biblical passage. It was my father's confession of the need of God's people. Nice, isn't it, if in the church you have a helpful "accountability" group or an opportunity to send the youth to summer camp or a winter retreat? Yet we can get along without such optional extras. We don't even have to have a "praise team," heretical as that may sound. But every time my father preached he was opening up a passage of Scripture, and, by doing that week-by-week, year-by-year, he was saying to the church, "The Bible is what you need." I think that has finally impressed me.

The second moment consists of a brief conversation my mother had with me as a lad. I don't remember the context; I simply recall that she was talking with me about the inspiration of Scripture (in terms a ten-year-old might understand). She said the Bible has such a richness about it, that you can go back to the same passage time and again and still see fresh truth there that you had not seen before. That, by the way, is just what you'd expect of something if the living, fascinating, interesting God was behind it. I've never forgotten that moment: she taught me to expect to meet the depth of Scripture.

Still another moment came at a Bible conference in Winona Lake, Indiana. I was probably in my early teens. It was a 7.00 a.m. meeting with Dr. Walter Wilson, a physician and Bible teacher who was likely in his seventies at the time. He stressed that in personal Bible reading you should continue reading (even if it took a long time!) until you found something you could use for that day. One has to be careful with that principle – you dare not twist the Scriptures in order to 'make' them practical. But his positive point was: don't simply read to read or to amass biblical data but keep asking how what you are reading applies to you and your circumstances. He made me assume the usefulness of the Bible; he was trying to tell us Paul was right: "All scripture is God-breathed *and profitable.*"

My fourth moment was a bit more painful, at least at the time. When I was fourteen, our family moved. In the middle of a school year. It's happened to other kids, but this time it happened to me: I went from the familiar and comfortable and enjoyable to the reverse. The new high school was strange and I was immediately behind in several subjects. Worse (to me), the whole area was a different kind of 'culture' and students at school didn't seem especially cordial to Christians. I am sure, as I look back, that I exaggerated the problem. But still, every day was a piece of misery. When I went to school I felt like I was going off to battle. No surprise then that I found the Psalms so sustaining. Early in the morning I would take my red, ball-point pen and underline texts in my Bible. One day it might be Psalm 56:9 ("This I know, that God is for me"), or maybe 57:1 ("In the shadow of thy wings I will take refuge, till the storms of destruction pass by"). Here I learned not merely the applicability but the urgency of the Bible. Day by day I dragged myself to the bus stop fortified (I hoped) by some fresh assurance from the Psalms.

Those are my "milestone" moments in regard to the Bible. Over the years they have, I think, produced a kind of desperation in me. The Scriptures in which God speaks to me have become the manna of my soul, and I find that I must have that "morning by morning".

David Robertson

David is a columnist, author, broadcaster and pastor of St. Peter's Free Church of Scotland in Dundee. He is the Director of Solas Centre for Public Christianity.

The young man was very confident in his understanding and rejection of the Bible. Too confident. 'Surely you don't believe in a book written by a bunch of illiterate desert shepherds? The Bible is a lot of rubbish'. He was also illogical (how could illiterate people write the Bible?!). I asked him if he had actually read the Bible. No – he had just read about it on various atheist websites. So the answer was simple. Why not just read the Bible?

I was brought up with the Bible and at one point in my teen-age life I suspect I would have sided with my atheist antagonist. But then I met some people who not only read the Bible, they said they believed it and it seemed to make a difference. So I started again.

As a sixteen year old I began reading at 1 Kings – not the best place to begin. I ploughed into 2 Kings and was on the point of giving up, when after a series of events, I became a Christian. I saw the Bible in a whole new light and for the past thirty-two years have read it through at least once a year. For the past twenty-five years I have taught it three to five times every week!

So what does it mean to me?

Firstly, it is an astonishing book – unlike any other. It is not an academic book yet is stretches my mind and makes me think unlike anything else I have ever read. It is not a self-help book yet it has been a greater help to me than everything I know. It is not a religious book and yet it has led me to God. It is not a political book and yet it has shown me why our world is in such a mess. It is not a book of morals and yet it has helped clarify for me right and wrong. In other words the Bible is my food and drink. I do not read, study or preach it as a 'professional' just doing my job. It is the Word of God. Through it God speaks not only to me, but also to his Church and indeed to the whole world. People are 'born again ...through the living and enduring Word of God' (1 Peter 1:23).

Indeed even as I write I have just returned from visiting a young man in prison, who having found himself in a cell on his own, began to read the Bible, and as he read Matthew's Gospel, experienced in himself a profound change. The Bible brings light into darkness, life into death and love into damnation.

Of course there are great difficulties in the Bible – what else would you expect? There is variety of genre, apparent (though not real) contradictions, and even the apostle Peter found some things hard to understand! But as the living and enduring Word of God, it is still as fresh and dynamic as the day it was first revealed.

The young friend that I mentioned at the beginning, decided to go and read the Bible. My last letter from him stated that he was now beginning to understand and it scared him that it all seemed to make sense. Indeed it does ...

Emma Mackenzie

Emma is a trained nurse with a masters degree from Queen Margaret University College, Edinburgh. She now lives with her husband on the family farm in Easter Ross, Scotland.

The Doctor sitting opposite to me simply said, 'I'm sorry. Your MRI scan has shown that you have multiple sclerosis.'

My fiancé put his arm around me as the tears started to fall. Our wedding was planned to take place in a couple of months. What about the future? What were we going to do? All we could do was pray and ask God for help from his Word, the living Word – the Bible.

So, what does the Bible mean to me?

It means many things but one of the most precious is that this is where I find God's promises.

We read in the Bible that when Jesus died on the cross and rose after three days the curse of sin was broken. As a result of this, if we, with the help of the Holy Spirit, ask for forgiveness for our sins and put our trust in Jesus then God has promised that he 'is faithful and just to forgive us our sins and to cleanse us from all unrighteousness' (1 John 1:9 NKJV). This is because 'God so loved the world that he gave his only begotten Son that whosoever believes in him may not perish but have eternal life'

(John 3:16). Once we have done this, as one of God's children, it gives us entitlement to grasp and hold on to all the other promises found in scripture.

When going into the tunnel of the MRI scanner I was scared, really petrified. I had big, not so glamorous, headphones on as the noise levels from the scanner would throb. Pop music from the radio filtered through and occasional instructions from the radiographer, but the only music I could hear was a Psalm I had memorised as a child,

Psalm 23
'The LORD is my shepherd ...
I will fear no evil for you are with me ...
Surely goodness and mercy shall follow me?' (NKJV)

The words went round and round, washing over me and giving comfort. These words learnt twenty plus years ago were there for me to meditate on and be used as a pacifier knowing that my God had inspired and promised them. This for me is the power of God's Word, it can come to you when you least expect it but need it most.

Many things have happened since the diagnosis that day. My vision has failed so that I can no longer drive. Sometimes my legs don't do what they are supposed to do, so I trip and fall. But the one thing that has stayed constant is God's promise of love and help which I can turn to again and again.

Scripture tells us how God commands and controls all things so that not even a sparrow falls to the ground without his will (Matt. 10:29).

We do not know what the future holds but our God does and if we wait on the LORD he has promised to incline his ear to our cry, to put a new song in our mouths and to set our feet on a solid rock (Ps. 40). All this is done as we wait patiently for Him. For me the Bible is a means through which God gives me the help I need and the instructions I require to do just that.

For Your Information

For millions, having the Bible in a printed format is of little or no help at all. This is an issue for those who can't read, are blind or deaf. Most live in the world's poorest countries and communities.

Bible societies and other Christian organisations have a commitment to ensure that everyone is able to personally encounter the Bible's life-changing message. This means that they will have to put the Bible into:

Audio – for the billion people in the world who can't read, and for those living in cultures where telling and hearing stories is the natural way to communicate.

Braille – for more than 800 million blind or visually-impaired people in the world.

Sign language – for thousands of deaf or hearing-impaired people whose natural way to communicate is in this expressive language.

Fiona Castle

Fiona is the widow of Roy Castle, the popular T.V. entertainer. She is an author and compiler of a number of anthologies. Fiona is involved with the Roy Castle Lung Cancer Foundation and also works to empower Christian women in seminars and workshops.

As a child brought up in the austerity of World War 2, going to church, singing hymns and psalms, listening to epistles and gospel readings were part of the normal routine of life at the time. It wasn't anything I particularly enjoyed, it was just something 'you did'!

The same could be said of school, where every day at assembly we sang a hymn, had a Bible reading and said prayers.

As I grew up, going to a boarding school from the age of nine where religion was a very important part of the school day, I suppose I was steeped in the rituals of Christianity all my life!

However, when it came to taking R.E. as one of my O levels, (as they were called in those days) I confess I found the Bible very boring. History was my worst subject at school, mostly because of the way it was taught, and Scripture seemed to fall into the same category. Oh, I knew the story of Jesus, and I believed in God. I could even quote many verses off by heart, but that was mainly so that I would pass my exams. It wasn't until I was thirty-five that the great awakening happened.

I was happily married, I had four children, with everything materially to make me content and yet I felt so unhappy and a complete failure.

One day a friend pointed out that although I believed in God and had gone to church all my life, I had never invited Jesus into my life. With her help, I took that step and immediately it was as if a whole new world opened up to me!

'Look, I am standing at the door and I am constantly knocking. If anyone hears me calling him and opens the door, I will come in and enjoy fellowship with him and he with Me.' (Rev. 3:20 TLB)

When I opened the door of my heart to Jesus, he changed my attitude to every aspect of my life. As I began to read the Bible and APPLY it, it worked!

'When someone becomes a Christian he becomes a brand new person inside. He is not the same any more. A new life has begun!' (2 Cor. 5:17 TLB).

There was, I discovered, so much in the Bible that talked about being a parent; bringing up and disciplining children; about marriage and about being a good wife!

As a result, our marriage changed; my relationship with my children became much more consistent and less dictatorial!

As I had a husband who was so often away from home, I had felt the weight of responsibility of keeping control of everything. When I released that into God's hands, I discovered that things didn't fall apart, but he gave me peace and security.

I have now been a Christian for more than thirty-five years and through all that time I have always found the answer I needed through reading God's Word – though not always the answer I wanted!

There must be an answer to every need under the sun in the Psalms. The important decision is to allow that Word to penetrate our hearts, to give us the peace that only he can give.

When my husband was dying and many were continuing, lovingly, to pray for his healing, I prayed – 'God, are you really going to heal Roy?'

Almost immediately I started reading 2 Corinthians 12 and these words jumped out at me,

'No, but I am with you; that is all you need.' These were words Paul heard, when he asked God to heal him.

I can vouch for the fact that he WAS with us and that he WAS all we needed to cope with the circumstances we were going through.

Jesus never promised us an easy life, but he did assure us that our future is secure when we trust in him.

'Here on earth you will have many trials and sorrows, but take courage, I have overcome the world.' (John 16:33 TLB)

Try it – it works!

Fred Apps

Fred is a long standing Artist and Illustrator. His talents are often put to good use in illustrating Bible characters and scenes in a gripping and realistic way.

There was a time when the Bible to me was just a book. One of those incomprehensible religious books full of people who think they have a duty to tell the rest of us how to live our lives. It was a book that I derided but sometimes dipped into out of curiosity to see what sort of crackpot tirades the finger waggers were aiming at us poor sinners outside the fold.

However, in my late twenties I became a Christian and had that amazing experience where verses were jumping out of the pages and socking me in the eye. I had an overnight conversion. Literally one day I was swearing like a trooper and living a typically worldly life and next day I walked into work with a Bible in my hand.

The Bible has become a book in which God reaches out to me. Once, having lived in a strict community, I went through a very bad time as a Christian and chucked it all in. For eight years I wanted nothing to do with Christians or God. I went back to many of my old ways. I didn't want to read the Bible because it all felt like judgement, except for Psalm 139, so

I only read that. Reading that psalm gave me a way back. It spoke of God's free and total love for me.

I see in the Bible so much about God's unconditional love for us. I know there are violent and bloodthirsty episodes, but I see in the Bible the amazing story of a God whose heart breaks over us and wants a deep relationship with me. It's taken a long time to learn this but I see it more and more.

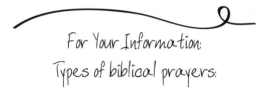

For Your Information:
Types of biblical prayers:

Confession (Ps. 51; Luke 18:10-24)

Praise (1 Chron. 29:10-13; Luke 1:46-55)

Thanksgiving (Ps. 105:1-7; 1 Thess. 5:16-18)

Petition (Gen. 24:12-14; Acts 1:24-26)

Intercession (Exod. 32:11-13; Phil. 1:9-11)

Commitment (1 Kings 8:56-61; Acts 4:24-30)

Forgiveness (Dan. 9:4-19; Acts 7:60)

Confidence (Ps. 23; Luke 2:29-32)

Benediction (Num. 6:24-26; Jude 24)

George Macaskill

George preaches for the Associated Presbyterian Churches in the town of Stornoway in the Outer Hebrides, a remote island community in the United Kingdom.

The Bible means 'truth' to me. I need something objective to rely on, and the Bible is that reliable, trustworthy source I can put my faith in – without fear. I do not trust myself. I cannot depend on my understanding of things, so it is very important, in the vital issues of life, that I have something reliable to turn to for direction. The Bible is that 'guide' to me. The Bible's evaluation of an issue is what gives me confidence. I know I can rely on the Bible's interpretation of everything.

I can rely on the Bible because it is a revelation from God. God is Truth. God sent us the Bible so that we would have something reliable to trust. Mankind has ruined itself and has run out of ideas. The Bible is God's remedy for the human race. The reason God gave us the Bible is that he wants us to know the truth.

The Bible is full of categorical statements and 'absolute' truths, and this strengthens me greatly. Truth is absolute! To say: 'There are no absolute truths' is, of course, an absolute statement in itself.

The Bible is also authoritative – which is why it is so un-popular. We need something to convict us and challenge us. The Bible does that to me.

It requires faith to trust the Bible, but it requires more faith to contradict it. The Bible is able to create faith in its reader, because God is its author. There is more reason to believe the Bible than any other book.

The Bible has not merely outlived us, but outlived all its enemies. No book is hated so much – yet it remains the world's best seller! The Bible defends itself. I love hearing of those throughout history who tried to eradicate the Bible but instead increased its production. I am tremendously encouraged to hear of so many people who have studied the Bible for the purpose of exposing its errors – and ended up convinced of its truth!

The Bible, however, is not merely for gaining true and accurate information – it is for finding Christ who is the truth. The Bible is how God communicates to us. God speaks to me through the Bible. If I want to hear from God, I don't try and go into a 'day-dream' – I go to read the Bible. If I pray that God will speak to me before I read the Bible, I always find that he does.

I personally find the Bible stimulating. It gives me life. I need the Bible to motivate me. The Bible wakes me up. The Bible thrills me; warns me; guides me; corrects me; encourages me; and strengthens me. Without the Bible I am lost, I am weak and I am hopeless. Without the Bible I feel life is meaningless and I am insignificant. I need the Bible to keep alive.

As I sit on my chair in my study, I have thirteen Bibles (in different versions) within reach. On my mobile phone I have nine versions and five Bible commentaries and dictionaries. I cannot live without my Bible.

For Your Information

A billion people in our world live on just sixty pence or just over ninety-six U.S. cents a day. That makes owning a Bible a luxury they can't afford.

It is also among these third-world communities that the Church is growing fast, for example, China, Nepal, Vietnam and parts of Africa.

These people urgently need Bibles. However some people such as refugees or prisoners will simply never be able to afford to purchase a Bible and must be given it free of charge.

Harry Reader

Harry is Senior Pastor of Briarwood Presbyterian Church in Birmingham, Alabama in the United States.

What does the Bible mean to me? In a word. Everything. Without the Word of God, I would not know the God of the Word. I am fully aware that God is revealed in creation, conscience and history but, I would not know the Triune God of glory without his revealed Word. I would not know why or how he made me. I would not know why or how he saved me. I would not know why or how he upholds me. But I do know, because his Word has told me that it is for the praise of the glory of his grace.

The Sovereign electing love of God the Father, the redeeming atoning love of God the Son, the effectual and powerful love of God, the Spirit, bringing me from death to life, I would not have ever known without the Word of God.

It was with the Word of God I was called from death to life. By the Word of God I was regenerated through the Holy Spirit from death unto life. It is through the Word that I have been saved from the power and penalty of my sins. I am being saved from the practice of my sins and I will be saved from the presence of my sins.

It is through the Word of God that my Savior not only speaks to my heart but frees my heart to speak to him with trust, confidence and love. I can speak to my LORD God about anything and everything upon my heart because of Him, who first loved me.

God's Word is alive and because of God's Word I know what life is and how to live life for him who loves me and loosens me from my sins.

As one theologian so aptly stated when asked how he knew that God has saved him, 'Jesus loves me this I know, for the Bible tells me so.'

I rejoice that the Bible is not a collection of truths but it conveys the truth in Christ. Every page, every text, every story, every law and every miracle recorded in the Word of God is there to point me to Christ.

The Bible is like the sweater that my grandmother knitted for me. It was knit from one thread and so it is with God's Word. No matter where you reach in and pick, it contains the one central message which is the Glory of God revealed in Jesus Christ as Creator, Redeemer and Sustainer. That is why I love to read it, I love to hear it preached, to meditate upon it, to hide it in my heart and to proclaim it to men and women that they might be brought from sin to the Savior, from death to life and from dust to glory. Most of all, I am thankful that the Word of Life, Jesus Christ has given me life through his Word. And with that Word, I might follow him who is now my life.

Helen Roseveare

Helen went to the Congo in 1953. She has dedicated her life to serving others even in the deep trials of life. Helen pioneered vital medical work in the rainforests of what is now the Democratic Republic of Congo, and is an international speaker with W.E.C. ministries.

As a school girl, the Bible came out once a week, in Religious Education class, when one of the teachers made us read a given passage and then droned on about it for thirty minutes – during which time, sitting in a back row in the room, I got on with my maths prep! I loved maths – it was my best subject – and I felt that dry old stories of long ago days were a bore. I had to listen just enough to be able to take the terminal test. The rest I ignored.

Then up at University as a first year medical student, I was lonely, and fearful. I had no friends: I was not in the top-ten, and found the studies hard: and I knew my father expected me to do well – I was scared to fail him. A girl invited me to her room one evening, and offered friendship. She showed me round the town, where to get a cheap lunch, and buy second-hand books. Next I went with her to a Bible study group – and for the first time in my life, I heard several of my own age-group discussing the Bible with obvious interest. I started to read with them. I began to become interested. I went to a house-party in the Christmas holidays. I sat, fascinated through daily Bible Studies, led by competent teachers, who obviously believed what they were teaching. For the first time I heard – really heard with my mind and heart, not just with my ears – that I was a sinner (Rom. 3:23), that I deserved death, God's judgement for all my wrong-doing (Rom. 6:23), but that God so loved me that he had sent his own beloved Son to die on the Cross of Calvary, in my place (John 3:16, Galatians). I could quote so many other verses!

Suddenly alive to my need of forgiveness, and love, and of a God who really cared, the last night of that house-party, almost in desperation, I threw myself on my bed, in tears and called out to God (if there was a God): 'Please make yourself known to me!'

Looking up through my tears, I read a text from the Bible painted on the wall above my bed: 'Be still, and know that I am ...' Psalm 46:10. However, the last word of the text had been washed out by rain through a leak in the roof! I was overwhelmed – GOD had spoken to ME! All the verses learned during that week suddenly fell into place and made sense – God loved me so much that he had sent his Son to die for me. It was true!

That evening, I fell in love with the Lord Jesus, my Lord and my Saviour. Within an hour, the leader of the Bible-studies at the house-party had signed me up to do a four-year Bible Correspondence Course that he ran – and through those studies, I fell in love with the Bible, the living Word of the living God. Since then, daily Bible reading has been my spiritual food through all the sixty-five years of my Christian life.

From the start I was encouraged to learn a verse by heart every week, and through the years that habit has paid wonderful dividends. When my back was to the wall in the civil war of Central Africa in the 1960s, terrified in the midst of hideous wickedness and cruelty, a phrase from a verse came (you might say, unbidden) into my mind: '(He was) led as a Lamb to the slaughter' (Isa. 53:7 NKJV) – and with the words, an amazing sense of peace. He, Almighty God, was actually inviting me to share in the fellowship of his sufferings – what a privilege! He was 'led to the slaughter' of Calvary for me, and he did not resist or refuse, so that I might be saved. Now he was inviting me to go through whatever might lie ahead, so that he could fulfil his purposes for those around me. Maybe God might not have given me that phrase, in the midst of such circumstances, had I not previously committed it to memory – but certainly it would have been hard to remind me of it if I had never put it into my mind in the first place! What a wonderful and caring God he is! And how powerful his living Word is at all times.

I cannot recommend too highly or too strongly the daily reading, learning, meditating in, feeding on and memorising of the Scriptures, the Living Word, the Bible. For me, they are the essential life-blood of Christian living. 'For me to live is Christ!' (Phil. 1:21 NKJV), and he is the Living Word.

Iain D. Campbell

Iain is a native of the Isle of Lewis, where he is minister of a congregation of the Free Church of Scotland. He is married with a grown up family. He loves reading and cycling, and has written several books.

When I was young, I read a story about a Christian girl who died during an operation. When her parents were going through her belongings, they came across a notebook in which their daughter had recounted some of her spiritual experiences. One of the passages of Scripture that was a great comfort to her – and to her parents, subsequently – was Isaiah 43:1-2 ESV.

'Fear not, for I have redeemed you;
I have called you by name, you are mine.
When you pass through the waters,
I will be with you;
and through the rivers,
they shall not overwhelm you;
when you walk through fire
you shall not be burned,
and the flame shall not consume you.'

I remember thinking, 'If these verses can speak comfort to a girl about to die, I want to have that too!' So I searched out the passage in my Bible, and it has been an inspiring passage of Scripture to me ever since.

Every time I read these words in Isaiah, I am reminded of three things. First, that the Bible speaks to us personally. I just love these words: 'I have called you by name ...'. This great book, written in specific situations to specific people, has a personal aspect to it that enables me to claim all its promises and rest on all its doctrines.

I don't mean by this what some modern theologians mean – that the Bible becomes the Word of God depending on how it affects me as I read it. But I do mean that in any given situation, the Word of God is applicable to me personally, as if God intended it for me and for no-one else. Its message is for me; its promises I can claim; its insights the basis for my hope.

Second, I am reminded that the Bible is alive. It is a living, powerful book. Its words have a transforming effect. Without them, we face operations, and a thousand other experiences, in our own strength. Yet the Bible, written over hundreds of years – as well as over hundreds of years ago – comes to us with an energy, vitality and relevance that addresses every situation in which we find ourselves.

I know of no other book like that. Other books give us memorable lines, wonderful insights and new perspectives on life. But the Bible demonstrates its power and strength by being not only the Word of God, but by being the voice of God into our souls. And it is still the case that the voice of the Saviour is able to calm the storm, heal the sick and raise the dead.

Jesus said of himself, as the Good Shepherd, that his sheep hear his voice, and as a result, they follow him and obey him. The Bible is where I hear that voice, and it draws me after the Speaker.

Third, I am reminded that the Bible speaks into our future. God's message through Isaiah was about a particular situation facing God's people – they were about to pass through waters, rivers, flame and flood. It was certain – God doesn't say, 'If you pass through the waters ...' but, 'when ...'.

In other words, he knows the future, and he plans our future. And it is precisely into the future that he knows that God speaks these words to us. Our future is not only known to him, but is addressed by him. When God made a covenant with David, David's response was, 'You have spoken also of your servant's house for a great while to come'. With a Bible in my hand, that is what I can say too. Whatever my past, or even my present, I know that God speaks in the Bible to me for a great while to come. My future is not dependent on my past, but on God's promise. So this great Book is more than a book. It is a personal word, addressing my particular situation, and giving me assurance for the rest of my life and for eternity too.

That's what the Bible means to me.

J. I. Packer

J. I. Packer is Professor of Theology, Regent College, Vancouver, Canada and was named by Time Magazine as one of the twenty-five most influential evangelicals alive.

The Bible meant nothing to me at all as a child. I was brought up in a churchgoing family and taught two prayers to say each bedtime, but my parents were not Bible-readers. Bible teaching was never discussed at home, and I had no Bible of my own until at sixteen I commandeered a stout, board-bound Edwardian King James Version that belonged to no one in particular, and began, off and on, to read it.

Why did I do that? An Austrian Jewish refugee family had come to our town, and the oldest and brightest of their three sons was a peer of mine in the sixth form, the school's top grade. He was a science student who argued vigorously for atheism, as at that time many well-known scientists did. I found myself propelled into championing the historic Christian faith (I had been reading some C.S. Lewis), and thought I had better get on terms with the Bible, to make sure I knew just what I was talking about. My reading, however, was spasmodic, and made no difference at all to the way I lived.

However, in 1944 I went up to Oxford, heard the gospel for the first time, and experienced the Lord Jesus Christ breaking in and reshaping everything. The group that discipled me stressed the importance of reading and meditating on Scripture daily as a means of communing with my Saviour, and they started me on John's gospel. The Lord Jesus was good to me, as so often to young converts, and knowing him through Scripture became a constant joy. And then, six weeks after my conversion, I went into a Bible exposition meeting assuming, as I had always done until now, that the Bible, wonderful as it was proving to be, was a mixed bag of wisdom and fantasy. I came out however, inwardly certain that the whole Bible, while fully human, was also wholly divine, and to be revered as such. I remember feeling bemused at the suddenness and strength of this conviction. It has never left me, and is part of my identity today.

First, then, I read and value the Bible as a letter, one that I re-read annually and parts of which I read much more often than that. Kierkegaard wrote somewhere: "When you read God's Word, you must constantly be saying to yourself, 'It is talking to me, and about me.'" That expresses exactly what I have in mind as I label my Bible a letter from my Lord. It is always and in all its parts, a divine communication addressed to me.

Second, I read and value the Bible as a listening-post, the place where I go to hear the voice of God through the Holy Spirit.

Third, I read and value the Bible as God's law, the standard for faith and practice, a model for praise and prayer, a compendium of wisdom for pleasing God and serving others, and thus a syllabus for saints.

Fourth, I read and value the Bible as a light in what it has led me to regard as the darkness of my life. Non-Christians often think of life as straightforward, but believers know better. Says Psalm 119:105 (NKJV): 'Your Word is a lamp to my feet and a light to my path.' See the picture! Life, yours like mine, is a journey across open, unfamiliar rough country. As we travel we are constantly at risk, for the terrain is treacherous and it is dark. The easiest thing in the world will be to stumble and fall over obstacles or into potholes that are invisible in the dark, and so do ourselves serious damage. We know that a path is there, but however much we screw up our eyes and glare into the blackness we cannot see it. We need a light and God in his mercy puts a flashlight into our hands. We shine it, and now we can see, not indeed our whole route, start to finish, but the next bit of the path, so that now we know where to put our feet. We walk without stumbling or falling. We move forward step by step towards our destination.

Walking by the light of Scripture is not like walking by daylight, any more than shining your flashlight ahead of you is like the sun coming up. Beyond the little circle of vision that the flashlight gives you, darkness continues to surround you, and it is through this darkness that we must travel as long as we are in the world. Which brings me to my final thought.

I read and value the Bible as my lifeline. Have you ever been near to drowning? I have, and in using this image I do not think I overstate. Deep down life has always felt frustrating in the way that the writer in Ecclesiastes describes. The proverb rightly says, while there's life there's hope, but the deeper truth is that only when there is real hope is there anything you can call real life. To moderns like me, drowning in hopelessness, disappointed, disillusioned, despairing, emotionally isolated, bitter and aching inside, Bible truth comes as a lifeline, for it is future-oriented and hope-centred throughout. The triune God, the Father, the Son and the Holy Spirit, is the lifeguard, who sees us drowning and comes to rescue us; and the Holy Scriptures are the lifeline God throws us to keep us connected with him while the rescue is in progress. The hope that Scripture brings arrests and reverses the drowning experience, generating inward vitality and joy and banishing for ever the sense of having the life choked out of us as the waves break over us.

Janet Mackenzie

Janet is a wife, mother and grandmother living in Perth-shire, Scotland. Over the years she has been considerably involved in reaching out to women through Bible studies.

Recently I had to spend a month in isolation in hospital undergoing some quite severe treatment, and with restrictions on the visitors to my room. One day my minister Alex came to visit me and brought me Psalm 91 printed out in case he wouldn't be allowed to take his Bible into the room. Psalm 91 begins, 'He who dwells in the shelter of the Most High will rest in the shadow of the Almighty.' It continues with many encouragements to trust God in the difficult times as well as the good times – just what I needed then.

The next day I received a text message from my friend Katie encouraging me with Psalm 91:11 'He will command his angels concerning you, to guard you in all your ways.'

A few days later dear friends Derek and Marion came to visit me and – you've guessed – Derek read Psalm 91 and talked me through it! Derek is a Gideon and a preacher. How good of the Lord to send me this encouragement when I was going through a rough time.

My family were not Christians when I was growing up, so, when as a fourteen-year-old I put my trust in the Lord,

I was put in touch with a dear lady called Barbara who lived nearby. She became my 'spiritual Mum' and I went to her each week for Bible studies. Barbara made the Word of God come alive to me! Her love of the Bible was infectious, and she encouraged me to memorise verses, which have never left me. She encouraged me from very early on to teach others what I had learned, and I have enjoyed leading Bible studies for ladies ever since. I particularly love to lead studies for those who have had little or no knowledge of the Bible before. To see how much joy it brings to people when they realise that God is speaking to them and that he loves them is such an amazing experience, and a real blessing.

God's Word is 'living and active' we are told in Hebrews 4:12, and it really is able to speak to us whatever situation we are in. But we do need to put in the effort ourselves, to read it regularly and to study it so that we can hear what God has to say to us, and so that what we have read will come back to us in times of need.

For Your Information

The first book printed with movable metal type was the Gutenberg Bible, printed by Johannes Gutenberg, before August 15, 1456, in Mainz, Germany.

The first complete English version of the Bible divided into verses was the Geneva Bible, printed in 1560.

Jeanette Sommers Wade

Jeanette is a freelance writer based in Birmingham, Alabama. She wears many hats ... mom, wife, equestrian, volunteer and she is an ongoing student of Denise George's writing seminars.

In the Bible there are songs, poems, laments, and instructions. It is a compilation of stories that describe people trying to make a living either with or without the one true God. The Bible contains comedy, drama and tragedy.

The Bible tells us in no uncertain terms that God wants us; all of us...heart, soul, mind, body. He wants you, your neighbor, your enemy and your friend. He wants the sophisticated and worldly wise. He wants the simple and plain. He wants the afflicted, the impoverished and the rich. He wants the selfish and proud. The wonder of God's grace is that he would want us for Himself. He doesn't need us; we do nothing for God; it is only his grace, love and mercy that makes us capable to accept Him. That is the wonder; we are given the choice to love him and we can only do that "because he first loved us". (1 John 4:19 ESV) We don't deserve this free grace, but it is granted, if we ask for it.

Therefore, the Bible means life to me. It is a love letter from God to mankind that in him is new life. We have to turn our self-made compasses over to him and let him be our true north. And this takes faith. Faith is belief that God speaks to us in the Bible. The Bible gives us hope that we have a Savior who gave up his life that we may have life. We must trust in God to guide us; to take our fears away. It takes faith to accept this incomprehensible love and mercy for us.

We are made in God's image; male and female. We are given emotions, personalities, and the inexplicable longing that is not satisfied in anything other than resting in Christ. This is where Christianity and other religions come to a crossroads. No other religion offers a Savior who rescues us from ourselves. Other religions may offer many things, but they don't offer salvation from our miserable self-striving to be god of our own lives. God does though. That is the life God intends for us.

For Your Information

About fifty Bibles are sold every minute.

The Bible was written by over forty different men who came from three continents: Asia, Africa, Europe.

The Bible was also written at different times covering 1,500 years by shepherds, fishermen, kings and people from many other walks of life.

Jennifer Grosser

Jennifer moved to England in her twenties to work with refugees. She moved back to the United States where she worked in a coffee shop getting to know the people of Worcester, Massachusetts, while writing her first book; *Trees in the Pavement.* She is now the director of Christian education at a community church there.

As a small child, I used to trundle into the sitting room while it was still early-morning dark, to discover my dad on his knees by the settee, with a Bible next to his elbow. I used to look at that Bible, pick it up, turn it over in my hands, wonder about it. There were so many words in there, and no pictures, but I knew that there were amazing stories in it. I knew it was about God. I knew Jesus was in that book.

When I had learned to read just a bit, my mum would let me look over her shoulder in church when the Scripture was being read, so I could read the same from the page. But her Bible was never the translation that was being read aloud, and I would get frustrated. Still, I knew there were amazing stories in it, and someone was reading something to us about God, about Jesus.

When I was older still, my parents gave me a Bible for my birthday. This one even had a few line drawings in it, and I could mostly understand the words, but I got stuck at Leviticus. Nevertheless, by this time I knew it was a book I was not going to be able to do without, and by the time I was a teenager,

I was making a concerted effort to read and interact with this amazing book on a daily basis. Or at least on a weekly basis. There were still things about it that utterly baffled me, but my dad said, "Keep a notebook and write down all your questions, and later we can sit down and talk about them."

I don't know that we sat down and talked about them all that much, but I still read the book and I still write down the questions or the amazing discoveries. The Bible itself says that it is "living and active" (Heb. 4:12), and that is something I have learned for myself as I have attempted to interact with it throughout my life. It is a vast book, sometimes intimidating in scope, but at the same time accessible to any age. The smallest child can understand the stories, and, interacting with them through her life, can find she is becoming part of the story, too.

Now I work as a director of Christian education for a community church. Many of the people there, in spite of having gone to church all their lives, have never once opened their Bibles. When we talk about it, they are afraid – afraid of what they don't know and afraid of getting started. But the Bible, for all its length and scope, is a very simple story of Good News of God's great mercy and forgiveness, and God caused it to be written so people would know. He designed for it to be looked at and held and wondered about, wrestled with and pondered and questioned. When we do that with the book he gave us, we come to find we also are doing that with him. He meets us in the pages of the Bible, at whatever age or spiritual state we are in, and speaks to us there. That is wonder indeed.

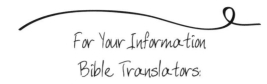

For Your Information
Bible Translators:

John Wycliffe 1328-1384
Known as the morning star of the reformation he was an early advocate for translation of the Bible into the common tongue. Wycliffe's translation of the Bible was completed by 1384.

Martin Luther 1483-1546
Luther was a German priest who initiated the Protestant Reformation. He taught that salvation is not earned by good deeds but received only as a free gift of God's grace through faith in Christ. His translation of the Bible into the language of the people (instead of Latin) made it more accessible and influenced the translation into English of the King James Bible.

William Tyndale 1494-1536
William Tyndale's aim was to 'cause the boy that drives the plough to know more of the Scriptures than the Pope himself'. William's translation of the scriptures had to be smuggled from Europe into England and it was because of his translation work that he was arrested and put to death in 1536.

Myles Coverdale 1488-1569
Myles Coverdale was a sixteenth-century Bible translator who produced the first complete printed translation of the Bible into English. He made use of Tyndale's translation of the New Testament and of those books which were translated by Tyndale: the Pentateuch, and the book of Jonah. Henry VIII had a Coverdale Bible put into every English Church, chained to a bookstand, so that every citizen would have access to a Bible.

Jessie McFarlane

Jessie McFarlane is the founder of Prayer Chain Ministries, a women's telephone prayer system and the author of *A Housewife's Adventure with God*.

One of the most precious words in the Bible for me is the word grace, and perhaps there is no sweeter, more beautiful word in human language than the word 'grace'. It has been described in many ways.

A little girl said, 'It is getting everything good, and for nothing.' But grace is more than that. Grace is everything for nothing to those who don't deserve anything. It's more than mercy, more than love.

For over sixty-six years, from the day I accepted Christ as my Saviour I have been the recipient of God's amazing powerful grace. Grace saved me from my sin at great cost, by God's grace he provided a substitute for my sin in the person of his own beloved Son, the Lord Jesus Christ. No wonder it is amazing grace!

Grace is the free favour of God in salvation. Someone has said it is 'God's unmerited, unrestricted, unrecompensed, and loving favour toward condemned and unworthy sinners'. This wonderful grace will go on and on. The apostle John wrote, 'And from his fullness we have all received grace upon grace'

(John 1:16 ESV). Not only did God save me by his grace, but he provides every spiritual blessing by his grace day by day.

A large sum of money was given to Rowland Hill to dispense to a poor pastor. Thinking that the amount was too much to send all at once, Hill forwarded just a portion along with a note that said simply, 'More to follow'. In a few days the man received another envelope containing the same amount and with the same message, 'More to follow'. At regular intervals, there came a third and a fourth. In fact, they continued, along with those cheering words, until the entire sum had been received.

C.H. Spurgeon used this story to illustrate that the good things we receive from God always come with the same prospect of more to follow. He said:

'When God forgives our sins, there's more forgiveness to follow. He justifies us in the righteousness of Christ, but there's more to follow. He adopts us into his family, but there's more to follow. He prepares us for heaven, but there's more to follow. He gives us grace, but there's more to follow. He helps us to old age, but there's still more to follow.'

Spurgeon concluded, 'Even when we arrive in the world to come, there will still be more to follow.'

I thank God for the wonderful privilege that is mine, in spite of my daily failures, that because of God's amazing grace, daily my shortcomings are forgiven and my relationship with God is determined, not by anything other than God's electing, redeeming and sanctifying love.

Jim Cromarty

Jim is a well-known author of both children and
adult books about Australia's great outdoors
and Christian history. He is retired and lives
in Australia. His story since retirement can be
read in *Stopped Work? Start Living!*

When I was asked to write this short piece titled:
'What the Bible means to me' I immediately placed
on my desk two Bibles that have always meant a lot
to both my wife and me.

My old King James Bible has the inscription: 'James Alexander
Cromarty, Primary School, 1945'. This was the first Bible I
ever owned. Although I now need larger print and read the New
King James Version, that Bible is very precious to me. That old
Bible is well marked as it was used by the Holy Spirit to bring
me to a saving knowledge of the Lord Jesus Christ. All my life,
even before I was converted, I looked upon my Bible as God's
inspired, infallible Word to me. It was through my reading of the
Scriptures that I came to see my sin, my coming judgement and
my need of a Saviour.

That old Bible accompanied me when I took up my first
teaching position in a small one teacher school in a remote
outback area of New South Wales, Australia. When I was met
by the family with whom I was to stay I was asked if I had a
'Protestant' Bible with me. When I replied in all innocence,

'Yes, I have,' I was told in very plain English, 'Don't bring it into this house.'

It was then I began to read that Bible as never before in an effort to discover why a person – a Roman Catholic – should speak in such a way about the Word of God which was so important to me.

In the twelve months which followed it was through the reading of my Bible that I became aware of God's judgement because of my sins. It was through my desperate reading of its pages that I became aware, as never before, that God had provided a Saviour. It was the Holy Spirit who drew me in saving power to the Lord Jesus Christ.

I read that Bible for many years and even though I have other Bibles my first Bible is still very precious to me.

The second Bible means a lot to my wife and in it is the inscription:

> Newcastle Teachers' College
> Awarded to Valerie Wood,
> for Needlework
> 1955.

This was the first Bible she ever owned and today it would be considered a most unusual request to be made of a book prize. This Bible became hers several years before she became a Christian, but again it was used by the Lord to point her to Jesus Christ, the Saviour of sinners.

What then does the Bible mean to me? It is the most precious book I have as it is God's letter to me; a letter that I read and reread. I continue to discover new truths as I read and pray that the Bible will again soon become the book that all sinners delight to read. By the grace of God they too will discover the Lord Jesus Christ as the Saviour of sinners and become faithful servants of the eternal, holy God.

The Bible has told me a lot about myself and the Lord Jesus. It has given me an assured hope that 'the best is yet to be'.

Since those days I have read many books – but as the chorus says:

> The best book to read is the Bible.
> The best book to read is the Bible.

If you read it every day,
It will help you on your way.
The best book to read is the Bible.

For Your Information

Today about 340 million people do not have the Bible in their own language.

John Huffman

John Huffman is Chairman of the Board of Christianity Today International. Prior to his retirement in 2009 John was Senior Pastor of St. Andrews Presbyterian Church, Newport Beach, California for thirty-one years.

What the Bible means to me is my very survival as a person! There are many definitions of the Bible. One of my favorites is: 'The Bible is the only infallible rule of faith and practice.' That is precisely what it is for me. I tells me all I need to know about God, myself and other people. It doesn't tell me everything about God, myself and other people but enough to get along with God, myself and other people.

Paul reminds young Timothy to continue in what he had learned and become convinced of. This is because of the godly persons who had instructed him in biblical teachings and "... how from infancy you have known the holy Scriptures, which are able to make you wise for salvation through faith in Christ Jesus" (2 Tim. 3:15). The Bible has done just that for me. It has made me wise unto salvation. Without the Bible I would have no reason to be convinced that God is a God of love who actually came in human form and died on the cross for my sins, rising from the dead in victory over sin and death. That's the "Gospel," the good news that there is nothing that I have ever done or could ever do that is unforgivable, except for one thing. That one thing is to quench the Holy Spirit, to say a final "no" to his pleading invitation calling me to repentance and faith in Jesus Christ alone for salvation. This salvation has two primary functions. One is "justification," that process in which I am made right with God and "sanctification," that process in which all my life I grow in my relationship with the Lord. In this and many more ways the Bible tells me about the nature of God and how I can come to peace with God. I have claimed the peace which passes all understanding ever since I received Jesus Christ as my Savior at five years old. And I have claimed that forgiveness and daily personal relationship with God.

But the Bible offers more than salvation and a continuing right relationship with God. It also helps me to get along with God, myself and others. I like the way Paul states this to young Timothy as he writes, "All Scripture is God-breathed and is useful for teaching, rebuking, correcting and training in righteousness, so that the man of God may be thoroughly equipped for every good work" (2 Tim. 3:16-17). All my life I have needed to be taught more and more from the Bible. All my life I have needed a biblical rebuke that confronts me with changes needed in my actions and attitudes. All my life I have needed the correcting that comes from the daily reading of God's Word, as painful as that correction may be. And all my life I have needed continuing training in righteousness that I might be thoroughly equipped for every good work.

To put it bluntly, I've learned that when the Bible says to do something, I better do it. If the Bible says not to do something, I better not do it. And on those matters on which the Bible is not quite so clear, my very daily exposure to it, at least in principles and attitudes learned, shapes me into the person God wants me to be. Thankfully the short-fall is covered by God's grace!

For almost thirty years now I have read the Bible all the way through each year. I've been the ultimate beneficiary of God speaking to me through his Word shaping me in both my faith and my actions.

For Your Information
Bible Translation Statistics

6.5 billion+ is the population of the world.

6,900+ is the number of languages spoken in the world today.

Almost 2,100 is the number of languages without any of the Bible.

340,000,000+ is the number of people who speak the 2,100 languages where translation projects have not yet begun.

1,668 is the number of language communities which have access to the New Testament in their language.

457 is the number of language communities which have access to the entire Bible in the language they understand best.

John Urquhart

John Urquhart was brought up on the Isle of Harris and studied at Glasgow School of Art. He then joined the BBC as a Radio and T.V. presenter before studying for a Divinity degree at Aberdeen University. He has been a minister since 1996 and now lectures in Sabhal Mòr Ostaig, the Gaelic College on the Isle of Skye. He is married with three children.

When I was eighteen and leaving home in Harris, for Glasgow, my step-father turned to me and said, 'Take this with you,' as he gave me a Bible. His gift then remained hidden and unread in my clothes drawers for the next few years as I moved from various halls of residence and lodgings.

About six and a half years later, after being asked to attend a Sunday morning Gaelic service in St. Columba's Church of Scotland, I was converted. It was only then that I felt a sudden and strong urge to root out this still pristine book and begin reading it. It amazed me then and has continued to do so ever since.

The importance of the Holy Bible cannot be over-estimated in its' ability (under the anointing of the Holy Spirit) to challenge, mould and alter thinking. I can still remember the utter amazement I felt when, just a few weeks after my conversion, our Minister, Jack MacArthur, preaching out of the Bible, told the congregation that Jesus was God – the second person in the Holy Trinity. I had to check what he was saying in my, by now, open Bible... and sure enough there it was, 'and the Word was God' (John 1:1). I was amazed that God would so love an undeserving sinner like me that He'd sacrifice himself to save both me and countless millions others like me. At that time I thought I'd have been happy enough if He'd sacrificed a great human for this purpose. But Himself! This was enough to bring the tears to my eyes. Since then the Bible has taught me that a mere human wouldn't have been enough to save us. He had to be perfect. Jesus, the God-man, was.

Now that I have been reading the Bible for the past twenty years, it still challenges, moulds and alters me. In fact I believe in the Bible so much that I'm on a small committee which is currently translating the New Testament into my own language – contemporary Scottish Gaelic. It's a privilege to be doing what Jesus did with Mary Magdalene after he rose from the dead.

In John's Gospel we see that the writer refers to her as, 'Maria' (John 20:11) in Greek – his own language, but he then records that when Jesus addressed her he called her 'Mariam,' (John 20:16) in Aramaic – her own language. He spoke to her in her own language to bring her to the knowledge of resurrection life, and this is a vital point. All of the world's peoples likewise need to hear the Word of God in their own native tongues. And I am glad, eternally glad, that I have heard and continue to hear it in mine. I thank God for the Holy Bible – which is no longer hidden away, but the open Book in our home.

Jonathan Carswell

Jonathan helps run www.10ofthose.com – a ministry that distributes trusted Christian books and resources at low prices.

I guess it is fair to say that we all search for God at some point in our life. We ask rhetorical questions (i.e. How can a God of love allow such horrible things to happen?). We investigate different faiths, or we attempt to be good in the hope that it will please God.

As a Christian I have come to find that I can have a deep, personal relationship with Almighty God. He is not a distant, uncommunicative God that is too busy for little me, a mere human. Instead, He is a God that draws near; a God that makes the first move so that even while I'm distant, and sinful in his sight, He comes to rescue me.

God makes himself visible in so many ways. Stopping to take in the world around us is one way we learn of God's colourful character. For me however, God's Word is central to how I interact with God and learn about him and eternity. Reading and meditating on it is like being on a drip in hospital – it feeds me with the spiritual goodness I need to live for him each day. Without it my spiritual life would rapidly die.

For sure there are bits that I find hard to understand, but each time I read I discover new things of God that astound me. Even familiar verses and stories have such depth to them that as I re-read them God shows himself to me in new ways.

I will be forever grateful to God that he didn't just leave us to fend for ourselves. Instead he gave us his Word and his Spirit to help us understand his Word. It is central to my faith because it teaches me of Jesus, who has done everything for me.

Linda Finlayson

Linda is a children's author. She brings together her love of books, children and history to write books about real people. Her latest book is entitled *Guarding the Treasure: How God's people preserve God's Word.* Linda is married to Sandy Finlayson and they have one son.

When I think of God's Word, I think of people; people whose stories populate the scriptures from Genesis to Revelation. They are people who have met with God and seen his handiwork in their lives, for good or ill.

When I was a child I loved to hear and read Bible stories. They were exotic and exciting. And I learned early that God was strong and able to change what seemed like impossible circumstances in a glorious way. Gideon's story always intrigued me. He was confronted with both an enormous invading army and God's battle plan, which included using the strangest of strategies and weapons. Gideon struggled to believe that God knew what he was doing and ended up with an amazing result.

God's strength and power was seen in Moses' life right from the beginning, when God protected him from the Egyptian soldiers in a small woven basket. And God went right on protecting Moses throughout his life, leading and teaching him so he could lead and teach God's people.

There were also stories that came with warnings. Jonah's disobedience led him to be dinner for a very large fish, and God could have left him there because Jonah deserved it. Instead God showed his mercy and compassion when Jonah prayed, asking God to deliver him. But then there were those who began well and ended badly. King Saul was chosen by God to be Israel's first king and at first Saul served God. But when Saul grew arrogant and disobedient, God deserted him. God was justly angry and offered Saul no forgiveness.

The stories of Jesus' life on earth are especially interesting and important to me. As a child I wondered what it would have been like to be in the crowds that listened to Jesus teach or watched him heal people. It must have been amazing and yet fearful too. Jesus looked like any other man, but he was also God's Son. What would it have been like to see his suffering at Calvary, or meet him after his resurrection? Which disciple would I have been like?

Through my years of growing up and growing older I have returned again and again to read the stories of Biblical characters. I find it comforting to read about people who were not perfect, yet God was merciful to them. Like me, Peter struggled with trusting Jesus, or managed to get it all wrong and was rebuked by the Lord. Like me, Job had to learn that God doesn't have to answer the 'why' questions and we must be content with that. Like me, David sinned, with grievous results, pleaded for forgiveness and received it. These stories give me comfort knowing that such people struggled just as I do and God was gracious to them.

The main reason I love the Bible stories is they teach me more about God than they do about the people. They reveal his attributes, his great majesty, his compassion, and his mighty power. Most of all they show me that God is all-wise and in control of everything. I'm reminded of that every time I read the life of Joseph. His life was a huge roller coaster ride. He began life as a favourite son, was then sold as a slave, became a trusted overseer, was falsely accused and imprisoned, and finally became the second most powerful man in Egypt. Yet all of these things happened according to God's plan and as a result Joseph was able to say to his brothers near the end of his life: 'you meant evil against me, but God meant it for good' (Gen. 50:20 ESV).

Lorraine Gosling

Lorraine is a wife to Anthony and mother to James and Matthew. When she is not looking after them, she loves reading, keeping in touch with friends all over the world, walking Wanda their dog, running, caring for mums and their babies as a midwife and enjoying God's creation.

As far back as I can remember the Bible has always been in my life. As a small child my parents would read it to me every day, it was something we just did. I loved to hear the stories and the characters I grew up with felt like people I really knew.

At Sunday School we would 'draw our swords' which was a very enthusiastic competition to see who could find a Bible verse first. It was a great way to learn how to find my way around the books, chapters and verses of the Bible.

Through God's grace as I continued to read his Word, I began to realise the Bible was more than just a book full of stories. It really was 'God's Word'. It was how he talked to me. It was how I got to know him. It was how I got to know about my real self and all that he had planned and promised for my future if I would turn to him and live for him.

'For I know the plans I have for you, declares the LORD, plans for welfare and not for evil, to give you a future and a hope' (Jer. 29:11 ESV).

In its pages I saw myself for who I really was, a sinner lost and ruined, but also the enormity of God's love was so clearly demonstrated to me.

For me the Bible has become part of who I am! When you are obsessed with something or someone you cannot get enough of it, you want more and more, whether it be a football team or famous person! It makes you feel good; it makes you feel like you belong. This is what it is like for me when I spend time with my Bible, God is there talking just to me. My son recently said to me that he was willing to listen to God. He went on to say that he had not heard him talking to him yet. I pointed him to the Bible where God's voice is never silent and can always be heard. I prayed that the Bible might have the same effect on him as it did on me.

There have been many people who have had an impact on my life who I greatly value and thank God for, however there is no one so reliable than my ever-loving unchanging Lord who daily continues to reach out to me through his Word and shape my life.

Malcolm Macinnes

Malcolm has spent the last twenty-two years ministering to the needs of a congregation now based in Kingsview Christian Centre in Inverness, Scotland. He is a husband, father and grandfather and has recently retired from pastoral ministry, but still preaches as often as he can, whenever the opportunity arises, and energy is left!

There was a time when the Bible meant little to me, and had little influence in my life. Times have changed. The Bible has not. I have. For me, the Bible is now the most important book in the world, and I pray that the Holy Spirit will increasingly shape me and my life by its teaching.

I think of the Bible's effect in my life in the way the Bible describes itself as a seed, a sword, a hammer and a light. There are other ways also, but I will comment on these ones listed.

SEED THAT IS SOWN.

When I read the Parable of the Sower, I conclude that I am like all four types of hearers. I have had times of being hard-hearted so the Bible message lay on the surface, not effecting any change in my life. I have been the 'rocky ground' when I felt some joyful response to the message being preached, but it did not last long in the face of opposition, from whatever source. I have been the hearer in whom the Word of God was choked by the pressure of other things. Thankfully I have been the 'good ground' hearer in whom the message of the Bible has had a saving effect. I thank God for that. The Holy Spirit has brought about in me the 'born-again' experience spoken of in 1 Peter 1:23, so that I have been born again through the abiding Word of God, the incorruptible, imperishable Word. Spiritual, saving experiences can exist only where there is spiritual life first, and that life begins in being born again.

SHARPER THAN A TWO-EDGED SWORD

The penetrating sharp point of a sword, and its cutting edge, are painful. The surgeon's scalpel exposes, and helps remove what is harmful to life. The Bible has been the same in my mind, heart and life as it exposes my sin. This has led to confession to God, and the experience of forgiveness and peace. Jesus said that when the Holy Spirit comes he convicts of sin, righteousness and judgement. I thank the Holy Spirit for beginning that work in me. This has not been a one-off experience, but an ongoing recurrence leading to conviction, correction and conversion to Jesus and a closer walk with him.

GOD'S WORD IS A HAMMER

The idea here is of breaking what is hard. The Bible has had that effect on me. The human heart is plagued with pride and resistance to the truth of God. Pride gets in the way of grace and humble dependence on God. I have learned that what the Bible says is true, that human effort and energy alone are inadequate to the work. There is an amazing truth recorded in Isaiah 66:2: 'This is the one to whom I will look: he who is humble and contrite in spirit and trembles at my Word' (ESV). These are words which the proud, self-sufficient heart cannot grasp. Yet, I thank God for them, and thank him for leading me into understanding their message.

YOUR WORD IS A LIGHT

The Bible describes the human condition as one of darkness, meaning that we do not know God, nor indeed are we capable of knowing him unless he intervenes. In the New Testament that intrusion of grace is described as God shining in our hearts 'to give the light of the knowledge of the glory of God in the face of Jesus Christ' (2 Cor. 4:6 ESV). For years I was exposed to Bible texts and messages, but they meant very little to me. Things have changed. God shone the light, and now I find that the Bible message impacts my mind, heart and life. I have come to hold Biblical convictions, and, for the most part, have been given, by God, the courage to stand by these. Many of these 'encounters' with God are registered in my memory as significant stages in life. I resisted the call to Gospel ministry until one day in a tenement building in Glasgow, I fell on my knees with the words of Paul in 1 Corinthians 9:16 etched into my mind and heart. 'Woe to me if I do not preach the Gospel' (ESV). That Scripture and that day settled the rest of my life. I believe that God who inspired the Bible gives times in life which will be remembered forever. For me, that day in Glasgow was one of these.

Mike Johnson

Mike is a lecturer at Cardiff University and studied Advanced Learning Technology at Lancaster. He lives with his wife and family in Wales.

Grace unto you, and peace, from God the Father and our Lord Jesus Christ. This phrase by Paul, addressed to the church at Thessalonica in A.D. 54, is one of those introductory verses we often skip, as we pass on to the 'meat' of an epistle.

'Grace' means 'unmerited favour'. If someone was unkind to you, and you were kind in return, that would be grace. As we strain to adjust the focus to God's grace in order to obtain a correct view of our state in sin, we should see that any favour shown towards us, rebels, iniquitous as we are, is far above anything that could be imagined issuing from a human heart.

No doubt Paul could act graciously to these people he had recently visited. But any other name, including Paul's, would empty the verse of any real use to readers. As great as it would be to receive grace from Paul, he died long ago. Even when he was alive, Paul could not be everywhere at once. God, being everywhere, and eternal, is actually present with me while I read the words, even in the words. It is a wonderful, vital, powerful truth to me that the simple words on the page actually convey God's grace to me, almost 2,000 years after they were written to these Thessalonians. The words remind me of gospel blessings: Jesus' perfect obedience to God's law counts for me, just as the dreadful punishment my sin deserves was borne by him on Calvary's cross. Reconciled to God the Father, I inherit an eternal home with him and all his saints. But the words are more than a reminder; they are alive through the Holy Spirit and give me sweet moments of fellowship with my gracious Friend, whom to know is life eternal.

I have tried to take Rev. Jim Elliff's parenting advice with my four children: he suggested taking them off, one at a time, 'into the wilds' to spend quality time together. The first to get this treatment was Padrig, then aged ten. In May 2008 he toiled up Pen-y-Fan, South Wales' highest peak, and then the clouds came over, pelting his face with hail. Through the sobs he began reciting Psalm 46, the whole of which we'd recently been learning. 'God is our refuge and strength, a very present help in trouble ...' (ESV) It was touching to watch and hear him draw courage in that way, but soon he would have a far more arduous trial to cope with.

In August 2008, we aborted our first camping holiday abroad, in France, because Padrig was in excruciating neck pain. The hurried return journey was harrowing. After being assessed by many different medical staff, Padrig was eventually diagnosed with medulloblastoma (malignant brain tumour). The operations, radiotherapy and a year of chemotherapy were very tough. In December 2009 Pads was scanned again and the result was clear. But five months later, he sensed a familiar feeling: a scan revealed that the unthinkable had happened. Against the odds, and to universal dismay, the tumour was back. More surgery, chemotherapy and radiotherapy followed. This time the chemo was so harsh that his own stem-cells were harvested to 're-boot' his immune system afterwards. Apart from the very lowest moments of agony, he really has not complained at all. God has sustained us. We have found his promises a sure soul-foundation. All the suffering is real. We are not stoics. The Bible communicates the grace of God which transforms pain into blessing. Pads still asks me to sing his hymn before the light goes out, 'Oh, the deep, deep love of Jesus'. Few there are who avoid the trials of this life, either for themselves or someone close. The Apostle Paul knew more than his fair share, but then he writes, 'I take pleasure in infirmities,' because they press home the immense and eternal blessings and benefits of being reconciled to our Glorious Maker through the gospel of our Lord Jesus Christ.'

Michelle Renihan

Michelle currently resides in Massachusetts, and has grown up in a home heavily influenced by Puritan theology. She has recently completed work for her M.A. in history, and looks forward to using her gifts to glorify God wherever he eventually places her.

I am a "rugged American individualist." It is with some shame that I admit this. Rugged individualism is not something Americans monopolize, yet it is something that has come to represent us to the world. We are "Americans" – full of Yankee ingenuity, self-reliant, brimming with confidence. The region of the United States where I dwell is full of these people, men and women who live their lives according to the code, "If you want something done right, you've got to do it yourself."

As children we are taught to trust in our own strength, and our own blood, sweat, and tears. In school, we learn to emulate those men and women who left their homes and set forth into unknown lands in search of freedom or out of a thirst for adventure. As we grow into adults, we place even greater trust in ourselves, because we learn – often the hard way – that people will let us down.

How often we forget the One who is truth and whose Word is true. God himself. As the Bible reminds us, God has already done what he promised. The God of the Bible is not a sinful, fallen human being; he is a holy, perfect God whose concern is the working out of his divine plan in this world. He is vastly superior to any other creature we have ever known, and we can come to Him, trusting he will care for us.

So many times in my life the Bible has brought me up short, reminding me that I can trust God to order everything in such a way that is for my good and his glory. Often I will come into the end of the school term and see the mounting exams and projects with a great amount of worry and stress. When I think about the future and what I will do upon graduating from the university, I get nervous trying to figure out where I should go and what I should do.

In Matthew 6: 25-34, Jesus, through the Scripture delivers a stern reprimand, telling me not to worry about the future, but to "seek first the kingdom of God and his righteousness, and all these things shall be added to you" (NKJV).

Other times I find myself absorbed in my own selfish interests, forgetting to spend time in prayer or in the Word of God, moving away from God and how he has said he is to be served by his people. Again, he calls me back; reminding me to turn from trusting my own strength and my own abilities to rest in him.

It is such a relief to trust God and his Word. As the writer of Proverbs recorded for us:

> "Trust in the LORD with all your heart,
> and lean not on your own understanding;
> in all your ways acknowledge him,
> and he shall direct your paths" (Prov. 3:5-6 NKJV).

And as the psalmist writes:

> "Many sorrows shall be to the wicked;
> but he who trusts in the LORD,
> mercy shall surround him" (Ps. 32:10 NKJV).

This has been such a comfort to me in my life. I can rest all my cares on an everlasting, infallible God who will make my way smooth and straight, who will help me glorify him in all that I do. If I am trusting God, believing what he reveals in the Scripture, and living my life according to his Word, then he will take care of me in ways beyond my human mind's comprehension. As Matthew records in the sixth chapter of his gospel, God provides sustenance for the sparrows and dresses the lilies of the field. How much more so will he care for us, his children, when we need his guiding care.

Trust is a wonderful feeling. I thank God that he taught this rugged American individualist through the Bible that she can lean on Someone infinitely stronger than she in order to live a life of honor and praise to Him.

Peter Nicholas

Peter was an Oxford rugby Blue, and currently works for Christians in Sport teaching the Bible. A 'Blue' is an award earned by sportsmen and women at university for competition at the highest level.

As a sportsman I must have heard it a hundred times, 'Good players do the basics well'. Throughout his time managing the England football team, Fabio Capello has emphasised that the team need to improve the basics: 'pass well, hold on to the ball, press high up the pitch'. Really, it seems almost too simple. Similarly it's something I need to remember about the Christian life. When Paul writes to the Thessalonian church – probably the church he was with the shortest time, and one of the congregations facing the toughest circumstances – far from telling them anything 'new' or 'here are the few things I didn't get to go through with you', he just re-emphasises the basics. 'We also thank God continually because, when you received the Word of God, which you heard from us, you accepted it not as the word of men, but as it actually is, the Word of God, which is at work in you who believe' (1 Thess. 2:13).

That's the challenge and the wonder of the Bible. It's a challenge to daily respond to it, as it really is, the Word of God. I find that there are lots of words in today's world vying for my attention; headlines, blogs, tweets, slogans – but if I am to live rightly in God's world what I need above all these other voices is to hear God's voice. It's also a wonder, that through the Bible by his Spirit God speaks to me directly and personally. I can know my maker and be known by him – what a privilege! Not only this but God's Word is active, it's at work in me as I believe – comforting, challenging, transforming, sustaining, refreshing me, and much more.

Far from being simplistic, keeping the Bible central to my life is incredibly profound – because in God's Word there is the most amazing dynamic. Day by day as I read scripture I see the life of Christ in all its glory. I see what perfection looks like, and I become deeply aware that I'm not the man I should be – that's humbling. And yet day by day I also see the glorious death and resurrection of Jesus Christ. It's my only hope for restoration and relationship with God, and I become deeply aware that I'm more loved than I ever thought I could be – that's restoring.

This is the core of the Bible's good news and it's this amazing message that is the 'basics of the Christian life'. And you know what? I never get bored of it because it's a truth that I'll never bottom-out, or exhaust. I've been marvelling at it for eleven years, and by God's grace I'll still be marvelling at it in eternity. As John Chrysostom, a church Father, put it, 'It is not possible, I say not possible, ever to exhaust the mind of the Scriptures. It is a well which has no bottom.'

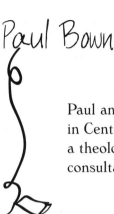

Paul Bown

Paul and his wife Kate were Christian workers in Central Asia, where Paul served as bursar of a theological college and then as an accounting consultant.

One of my favourite books of the Bible is Proverbs, written in part by King Solomon. Within its thirty-one chapters there is a wealth of ancient wisdom that supplements, informs and challenges contemporary 'good sense'. I love the English rendering of the more descriptive and evocative sayings. 'As a door turns on its hinges, so a sluggard turns on his bed' (Prov. 26:14), brings to mind a hapless vagabond, tossing and turning under his bed clothes, failing to find rest, but too lazy to get to work.

The same spirit may avoid rising from slumber by exclaiming, 'There is a lion outside!' or, 'I will be murdered in the streets!', (Prov. 22:13) and may find eating too burdensome to attempt, 'The sluggard buries his hand in the dish; he will not even bring it back to his mouth!' (Prov. 19:24).

The tantalising appeal of gossip is clearly described, 'The words of a gossip are like choice morsels; they go down to a man's inmost parts' (Prov. 18:8), but warnings are given about spreading rumours, 'A perverse man stirs up dissension, and a gossip separates close friends' (Prov. 16:28).

I lived eighteen years in a culture steeped in the tradition of the 'elders', much like the culture of Solomon's time. I needed the 'hands-on' wisdom of Proverbs each day as I faced many demanding and bewildering choices and decisions. Most days my wife and I were faced with demands for loans or financial help. As I turned to scripture for guidance I found the very uncomfortable words, 'If a man shuts his ears to the cry of the poor, he too will cry out and not be answered' (Prov. 21:13) and the encouragement, 'A generous man will prosper; he who refreshes others will himself be refreshed' (Prov. 11:25). We still needed to exercise great wisdom as to when to give or to refrain, but we found much blessing in hearing the 'cry of the poor' and responding where possible.

Many times during the long, hot and sticky summers, it was very tempting to gravitate under the ceiling fans, to enjoy the cooling downdraft and to put off venturing outdoors. When asked to visit an office to solve an accounting problem there were plenty of 'reasons' why I couldn't go at that particular hour. Perhaps it was the rush hour – the buses would be crowded and the journey long. Or perhaps there was tension in the city. Was it really safe to venture out? On those occasions Proverbs 3:27-28 would come to mind, 'Do not withhold good from those who deserve it, when it is in your power to act. Do not say to your neighbour, "Come back later; I'll give it tomorrow" – when you now have it with you'. I needed a stark reminder that I should do all that I could to serve my brother or sister in Christ on that day as 'tomorrow' is an uncertain reality. And often the journey or the tension in the city was not as bad as I had thought.

There are dozens of other maxims in Proverbs that I still chuckle at. Clearly Solomon and the other writers had a good sense of humour. To do justice to the scriptures we cannot pluck these sayings out of context as avowed promises to twist God's arm to bless us according to our perceived wants or needs. Rather, these adages are prescriptive, prescribing how to lead a life that God blesses. In our years of living overseas we saw many of our Asian friends prosper spiritually, if not materially, when they took the wisdom of Solomon to heart in their daily struggle to live honourably before God and men. 'The fear of the LORD is the beginning of wisdom, and knowledge of the Holy One is understanding' (9:10).

For Your Information:
The Books of the Bible

The Old Testament has seventeen Historical, five Poetical, and seventeen Prophetic books in it.

Seventeen Historical Books	Seventeen Prophetic books
Genesis	Isaiah
Exodus	Jeremiah
Leviticus	Lamentations
Numbers	Ezekiel
Deuteronomy	Daniel
Joshua	Hosea
Judges	Joel
Ruth	Amos
1 Samuel	Obadiah
2 Samuel	Jonah
1 Kings	Micah
2 Kings	Nahum
1 Chronicles	Habakkuk
2 Chronicles	Zephaniah
Ezra	Haggai
Nehemiah	Zechariah
Esther	Malachi

Five Poetical Books

Job
Psalms
Proverbs
Ecclesiastes
Song of Solomon

Rebecca Carlisle

Rebecca is from Georgia in the United States and has spent a life-time in education. Mother of two adult daughters, Sam and Shea, and wife of Richard, retired Elementary Principal from Ephesus Elementary. She has entitled this article: *The Bible Through the Eyes of a Child.*

The year was 1899 when the Gideon organization was founded. The Gideons have been placing Bibles in hotels over the past 100 years. They have placed Bibles in the hands of over 1.6 billon people. They believe that God uses his Word to change lives. Isaiah 55:11 says, "So shall my Word be that goes forth out of my mouth: it shall not return unto me void, but it shall accomplish that which I please and it shall prosper in the thing where to I sent it." The Gideons believe that the Bible contains answers to life's vital questions and can help everyone understand how to have a relationship with God. The Gideons have also placed Bibles in the hands of school children around the world.

The year was 1960 and I was a student in the fifth grade. Our teacher, Mrs. Handley, announced that the Gideons were coming to our classroom to give everyone a Bible. I couldn't believe that people would be so generous as to give everyone in our class the gift of a Bible. Later that day a man came to the classroom with a box of little red Bibles. The Bible contained the New Testament with Psalms and Proverbs. I didn't know who the Gideons were but they had to be special to give such wonderful gifts. We couldn't wait that day to go outside and read everything in the little red Bible. My friends and I would sit on the playground and take turns reading verses to each other. We wanted to see who could be the first to read the Bible from front to back. I couldn't wait to get home and show my mother the gift that I had received.

In the year 2010 I had just completed forty years in education. At the end of the school year I will be retiring from serving as a principal of a small rural school. I received a call from a friend who was a Gideon. He asked permission to come and give Bibles to our fifth grade students. I think back to how times have changed. The Gideons can no longer go into the classroom to present Bibles to students. All I can do is go to the classroom and tell the students that there would be a box of Bibles outside on the table for anyone who would like one. To my amazement and delight each student, without any coaching, chose to pick up a small red Bible on their way to lunch. I watched the excitement in the eyes of the students as they looked through their Bible. The students couldn't believe that they received such a special gift. I watched students getting into groups later that day on the playground taking turns reading the little red Bible. Times may change but children do not. Our desire to have a close relationship with God remains strong.

Rebecca Davis

Rebecca is a writer, teacher and storyteller who lives in Greenville, South Carolina. She has written several books for children as well as magazine articles for adults, and loves to speak about the Lord. She and her husband, Tim, have four children. She has entitled this article: *The Magnifying Glass of God.*

I was studying the Psalms, taking copious notes. If this was God's message to me, then you'd better believe that with all the determination I could muster, I was going to understand it. I wanted the Word of God to be my greatest delight. So I kept getting up early – studying, studying, studying. Learning, learning, learning. And glad to be doing it!

Honestly, though, it never even crossed my mind to ask God to open my understanding. He had given me a brain, and that's what I was using. After all, didn't somebody say that I shouldn't ask God to do for me what he had already given me the ability to do for myself?

Then I came to Psalm 22, the one all about Jesus dying on the cross. And the sad fact is that I wasn't interested in studying it.

I knew why. I knew exactly why. It was because it wasn't about me. Almost every other psalm so far had been, in my mind, about me. But I knew this one was important, and I knew it wasn't about me, and I knew that I wasn't excited about reading it.

I wrote in the margin of my wide-margin Bible,

12–2–1993
I'm struggling with the fact that I don't appreciate a Psalm
as much when it's about Jesus instead of me,
and what selfishness and immaturity that reveals.
Now I'm faced with a Psalm that can't possibly be
appreciated properly unless it's applied to Jesus.
God, grant me the grace to rejoice in your holy Word!

To look at it now, it seems ridiculous not to appreciate a passage about Jesus. But this was one of the first times in my life – if not the first time – that I actually asked God to open my understanding.

And I almost tremble to recall the results. Psalm 22 opened to me like Aladdin's cave. I came to tears again and again at the beauty and grace and outpouring of love I saw in my Savior. Beyond seeing him as simply my great example (that's how I kept referring to him in the first few days of my study), I began to see him more clearly as the ultimate Sacrifice: his sweat poured out, his blood poured out. As the ultimate Victor, singing the praise of God in the great congregation. As the ultimate Feast of his meek ones, the all-satisfying Living Bread. As the Great Accomplisher of the greatest Work. It is Finished.

This experience marked a turning point in my Christian life.

Through the years, I had thought of the Bible in a number of different metaphorical terms. A friend told me that too many Christians read it as if they're looking for a Daily Vitamin Pill. When I began reading for actual understanding, I thought of it as my Map from God, giving directions to him. I thought of it as my greatest Treasure.

Though it was years before I began to consistently cry out for the opening of my understanding every time I opened the Word, I began more and more to see the Bible as my great Magnifying Glass.

May my heart ever resound with unending praise to the Savior, the one to whom this Magnifying Glass points like a laser beam, the one who alone is worthy of all blessing and honor and praise and glory and power.

Oh, magnify the LORD *with me,*
and let us exalt his name together (Ps. 34:3 ESV*).*

For Your Information

The words, "Don't Be Afraid" appear 365 times in the Bible the same amount of days in the year.

Richard Bewes

Richard is an author and retired rector of All Souls Church, Langham Place, London. He is an experienced broadcaster, conference speaker and the author of more than twenty books.

Growing up as a child on the lower slopes of Mount Kenya I had everything I wanted – even though our clothes and toys were home-made, and our missionary bungalow was without gas, electricity, sanitation, telephone, running water – or taps. There were no shops nearby, no postal service and no doctor within twenty-five miles.

Yet we children were relating to the universe around us from day one. Early schooling – through my mum – took place on the verandah. And night time was story time! Most of the stories were acted out. Before I could read, we were learning about Noah and the Flood. 'Drip drop, drip drop ... pitter-patter, pitter-patter ... whooooosh ...!' We did Solomon's prayer for wisdom; we did Samson ... Zacchaeus ... Jeremiah down the pit ... the three loaves at midnight ... the burning fiery furnace ... Herod ... how Saul became Paul ... Jonah ... the tent-peg through Sisera's head – and story after story about Jesus.

If it's stories you want, the Bible is packed out with them! You don't even have to work at it too hard in forming a cohesive world-view. Bit by bit the big picture becomes assembled, and before too long you've got the four great planks of our existence in place – Creation, the Fall, Redemption and the End Times.

Then it is that you find yourself with a handle on virtually every human issue and perplexity going: wealth creation, education, race, sport, art, sex and the family, conflict and war, disaster and disease, death and the future.

And above all, it's Christ that the Scriptures have led me to; not the military Christ of the Crusades, not the superstar Christ of show business, not the social programme Christ of the modernists, nor the existentialist Christ of post-modernism but the true God-Man of the Bible, who came among us to live, die, rise and now rule – soon to return!

As I wake every morning, the thought arises – Another day of adventure on Planet Earth with the Lord Jesus Christ. Admittedly, the 'adventure' begins rather pathetically – with a cup of tea. But then as I pad upstairs again, I'm thinking that in a minute or two I shall be having a meeting – by agreed appointment – with Jesus Christ himself; why, in five minutes time I shall be eating honey out of the Bible!

On the day I write these words, I have been reading about the wicked king Ahab and his grabbing of Naboth's vineyard. Then I turned to the New Testament and I was in 1 Thessalonians 4; the passage about the Lord's return. This is the chapter that was read to my missionary dad during the very moments of his departure from this life, aged ninety-one. When you begin to apply all this to your relationship with Christ, to your present world you find yourself in prayer – and the day ahead.

We're like the travellers on the road to Emmaus (Luke 24:13–33), to whom the resurrected Lord explained, 'in all the scriptures the things concerning himself.'

Take that all out and we have no world-view that can stand up with any credibility whatever. As John Whittaker put it in his hymn 'Immortal Love For Ever Full':

> To turn aside from Thee is hell,
> To walk with Thee is heaven.

Rico Tice

Rico is co-author of Christianity Explored and is currently Associate Minister at All Souls Church, London. He is well known in the U.K. as a speaker at evangelical Christian conferences. Rico grew up in Uganda and Zaire, studied at Bristol University where he was captain of the rugby team. He married Lucy in December 2008 and their little boy Peter was born in October 2010.

There's nothing like the written Word of God for showing you the way to salvation through faith in Christ Jesus. Every part of Scripture is God-breathed and useful one way or another – showing us truth, exposing our rebellion, correcting our mistakes, training us to live God's way. Through the Word we are put together and shaped up for the tasks God has for us (2 Timothy 3:15-17 MSG).

If I'm pulling a book off a shelf, almost instinctively, as I handle it, I ask three questions:

Who is it by?
What is it about?
What is it for?

When I ask those questions of these three small verses in Paul's last letter to Timothy, written from prison, then they brilliantly sum up the 'absolute' importance this book has for my life.

I wonder if you look at the passage and ask these questions if you can see the answers? Have a go!

WHO IS IT BY?

Now hold onto your seats, can you see the devastating answer to that question: 'Every part of Scripture is God-breathed'. The word in the Greek is *theopneustos*, which means breathed out by God, as though it is on his breath. So this book is 100 per cent written by human beings, but it is also 100 per cent inspired by God. It therefore totally originated in God's mind. He decided what would go into it and then breathed it out by his Spirit through the authors.

And this is exactly how Jesus saw it, as God's Word. Now the application is mind-blowing. It means when I open this book this is God addressing me today. So do I want to hear God speak? Then I need to read the Bible and I'll experience God speaking to me. In prayer I then speak back to him.

WHAT IS IT ABOUT?

This book is about 'salvation', how to get right with God through Jesus. How to be saved from God's righteous anger at our sin, through the death of the Lord Jesus on the cross.

So the start of the Bible describes how God made the world and meant for us to live in relationship with him. But we turned our back on him. We rebelled. Nevertheless God had mercy on us and ultimately he sent his son to die, so we could be forgiven our sins and brought back into relationship with him.

Furthermore, Christ rose again and obtained for us eternal life. So he has saved us from sin, the consequences of sin and eternal death, and one day Christ will return to earth to rule from the judgement onwards.

The Bible pleads with us to link our lives with Christ, to come to him as our Master and Saviour. So the Bible is all about being saved through Jesus, it is all about trusting in Jesus.

As you come to any book of the Bible, the big question to ask is how does this book teach me to trust in and have faith in Christ? As Martin Luther wrote: 'The Scriptures are the cradle in which the baby Jesus lies'.

WHAT IS IT FOR?

The Bible tells me that its purpose is for me to be able to live a godly life: 'Every part of Scripture is God-breathed and useful one way or another – showing us truth, exposing our rebellion, correcting our mistakes, training us to live God's way. Through the Word we are put together and shaped up for the tasks God has for us' (2 Tim. 3:16-17 MSG).

So the Bible teaches me how to live and which way to go. When I am faced with decisions I go to this book. I may talk to Christian friends and ask them how the Bible can guide me so that I can make a godly decision. I can then ask God for the resources and strength to make that decision, however hard it may be.

So who is the Bible by? God.

What is the Bible about? Jesus and how to find the way to eternal life.

What is the Bible for? Godly living.

It couldn't possibly be more significant to my life, I'd just ask for your prayers that I make time to keep reading it.

Stewart Mackay

Stewart Mackay studied at Glasgow University and Highland Theological College and is now an Army Chaplain for the British armed forces. He is married to Maggie and they have a young son.

I came to faith in Jesus Christ shortly before my twenty-seventh birthday. Prior to that I'd spent some time looking for answers to questions such as: 'Why did war and conflict happen?' And, 'Why did people do such evil things to each other?'

It was after some friends shared Christ with me that I went along to church to check it out. I felt that I was already a little bit familiar with the Church of Scotland tradition, but not the Christian faith. When I opened the Bible that first Sunday evening in church it felt as though the lights were switched on for me spiritually. All the answers I had about life were to be found in this amazing book. And when I did come to hear some good biblical preaching it felt very much as though the Word of God burned deep within my soul.

I went on to study anthropology and some biblical studies in Glasgow University for a year. Whilst I was there I attended St. George's Tron church in the city centre. Although I wasn't sure where my studies would take me I felt impacted by the Word that was preached there. I transferred my studies thereafter to

Highland Theological College and was again thrilled at coming under some inspiring biblical teaching.

Several years later I responded to the call of God upon my life to enter into the ministry of Word and Sacrament and have since been ordained into the Church of Scotland ministry. Having served as an infantry soldier for five years after leaving school I vowed (to myself) that I would never return in any way, shape or form to the armed forces. That said, I now find myself delighted to be back in the armed forces again serving in the Scottish infantry, but this time as a non-combatant army Chaplain.

I'm here to bring Christian care of body, mind and soul to the soldiers wherever they are serving. As I write we are in Afghanistan. Although there is deep darkness in this part of the world just now, I feel thrilled at having the opportunity to reflect the light of the Gospel to these soldiers during their time of need.

The Word of God that first inspired me continues to do so. I read it almost every day and follow the Robert Murray McCheyne annual reading plan. It is engaging in a way that no novel is because no novel fills me spiritually the way the Bible does. It is intriguing in the way no other book is because there is always more to learn. And no other read gives me such an intimate sense of God's presence in my life. It is instruction on how to live. It is revelation of God's plan of salvation for humankind. It is food for the soul. And it's my prayer that it will become an inspiration to those God has called me to serve.

Suzanne Lofthus

Suzanne is the Artistic Director of Cutting Edge Theatre Productions which was formed in 1995 to contribute to the 'spiritual, social and economic vitality of Scotland' by producing works of high quality to be seen by a wide variety of audiences.

To me, the Bible is a textbook of creativity, relevance and truth!

CREATIVITY

As a Theatre Director, it's my job to dig underneath the words that are written on a page and this is fascinating when examining the Bible. For example, we read in the Bible only a short paragraph on the death of Jesus, so it's my job when working on Passion plays, to dig beneath that. Asking questions such as 'Who was there?', 'Why were they there?' and 'What did they feel like?' all take me (and others) deeper into the truth. Of course we can't really know what went on in the hearts and minds of those people but we can get close. And then when that is revealed to us, we reveal it to others.

It's a fascinating journey to read and then wonder at the lives and feelings of those who lived and walked with Jesus. So, something that happened thousands of years ago can still be translated into a work of creativity that makes a difference to us today.

God is a creative God and that creativity is woven through the Bible which in turn, inspires us creatively today.

RELEVANCE

The Bible is the living Word for today – so relevant, even though modern society would have us believe that it's out of date with no relevance whatsoever. I am constantly amazed at exactly how relevant it is and how anyone can identify with Jesus and find he speaks into their lives.

I was recently involved in setting up a Passion play in a U.S. prison with guys who were arrested (some unjustly), tried (some unjustly), and sentenced to death. When we spoke about Jesus, we realised he had experienced all that and more – so the guys were able to identify directly with Jesus and bring a whole new slant on the play.

In that prison I also heard an inmate Pastor preach on 'not just reading the Word, but acting on the Word'. That was a life changing moment. Here in a place where there would seem to be no hope, there is incredible hope! Here is where the rubber hits the road – there is no hiding in prison and no pretence. If you say you're a Christian, then others are going to look at you for the proof of that!

TRUTH

Having come through a spiritual crisis for four years, the one thing I kept going back to was – what did Jesus actually say? That is truth – he is truth personified! I heard a story during that time about St. Francis of Assisi who was faced with the Bible and came to the same conclusion – when Jesus says 'do not worry', he means 'do not worry'. No amount of arguing our case can justify. We either trust him or we don't – black or white! So get stuck into the Bible and find out how to live the Christian life. It's transforming! The Bible for me is the place where the rubber hits the road! It's the place where we find that Jesus knows, understands, cares and is relevant. He walks through every day with us, whether we feel him or not. Look in the Bible. He walks there through every moment. It's a place of inspiration, of wonder and of awe as well as the place of challenge! Let's not just be hearers of the Word though – let's be doers!

Catherine Mackenzie

The only way Catherine's parents could get her to take some detested medicine as a child was to 'bribe' her with a copy of a children's book on Gideon. Today she works as the Children's Editor at Christian Focus Publications in Scotland.

A book has to be read to have any impact but the Bible is different. God, as its author, is not limited to pages and text. He is the living Word and with that power his Word goes out into the entire world, into any heart and mind and gets to work.

The Word of God doesn't have to be bound between cloth covers for it to be powerful. It can lie dormant in the mind for decades and then reappear through a memory. You can hear it just once and it will change your life. It can come out of nowhere into your very being even if your culture doesn't have a Bible in its own language. God's Word has a life of its own because in a wonderful, mind boggling way, the very words we read from God are God.

When I was ten years old I read the opening line of Psalm 23 inside a golden locket. I had been looking for evidence of a romance, but instead I came across true love – the love of God. And that is one thing that the Bible means to me – love. It has shown me that God loves me and that I need to love God above all else and above all others. Not that my love makes God love me anymore than he does. To love more than he does already is not possible for God. He only ever loves completely. His love once given is never diluted, taken away or even withheld temporarily until we sort ourselves out.

If I were to go through the Word of God studying only one word, love, I would never get to the end of the wonders. In our world many search fruitlessly for unconditional love. But when we go to the Word, the one Word, the true Word – we will find that there is only one condition to true love – and that is to receive it from God in exchange for wickedness and sin.

I'd like to draw your attention to one particular passage of scripture that I think illustrates God's love in a truly graphic way. Look up Zechariah 3 in the Old Testament. It's a simple story about a swap.

Joshua the high priest stands before Satan and the LORD. He is dressed in filthy clothes and Satan is accusing him. The LORD rebukes Satan and in a triumph of grace takes away Joshua's filthy clothes and with that his sins. Now you'd be forgiven for thinking that God had done enough by taking away the problem of sin. But no – God, as the God of grace, desires to give abundantly and above what we could ever imagine. Joshua's sin is taken away with his dirty clothes and he is given in exchange new clothes, rich clothes, splendour, authority, respect, dignity and privileges. This is an exchange that can also be ours through Christ. Standing there dressed in the righteousness and glory of the Son of God we are fit for a heavenly royalty. Without the Bible I would never have known that this was a possibility. I would have remained hopeless, unloved, unforgiven and guilty.

I am thankful for those who told me about God's Word, read to me from it, sang and preached of it, printed it, translated it and even smuggled it through the years so that today I can read and understand its truth. But they are vessels and not the source. I am thankful to the Word for the Word! Thank you God.

BIBLE FACTS TIME LINE

255 B.C.	Translation of the Old Testament into Greek. It was called the Septuagint. This word comes from the word seventy in Latin and refers to the number of translators.
A.D.	
360	Scrolls begin to be replaced by books.
500	Most monasteries have manuscript copying rooms.
698	Lindisfarne Gospels begun (completed in 721).
845	Vivian Bible (early illustrated manuscript, written in Tours).
885	Alfred the Great translates Gregory's 'cura pastoralis' into English.
1382	English translation of New Testament completed under Wycliffe's leadership; Wycliffe expelled from Oxford, his doctrines condemned by the London Synod.
1434	Gutenberg invents moveable type.
1455	Gutenberg Bible printed (edition of Latin Vulgate).
1516	Erasmus published the New Testament with Greek and Latin text.
1521	Martin Luther excommunicated.
1522	Martin Luther completed the German New Testament.
1526	William Tyndale's pocket-sized New Testament reached England.
1530	William Tyndale's Pentateuch translation printed.
1534	Luther completed translation of Bible.
1535	Coverdale Bible by Miles Coverdale.
1537	Matthew's Bible (published under name of Thomas Matthew, but it was really the Tyndale translation with gaps filled in from Coverdale translation).
1539	Great Bible published and copies were given to every parish church in England.
1549	Book of Common Prayer published.
1560	Geneva Bible published by William Whittingham.
1568	Bishops Bible (revision of Great Bible) published and sanctioned as Bible for Church of England.
1611	King James Bible completed.
1661	John Eliot translated the Bible into the Massachusetts Indian language.
1801	Bengali New Testament completed by William Carey.
1804	British and Foreign Bible Society formed.
1809	William Carey published entire Bible in Bengali (5 volumes).
1816	American Bible Society founded.
1940	Wycliffe Bible Translators founded.
1978	New International Version published.
2001	English Standard Version published.

Are You New to the Bible?

Perhaps these stories have intrigued you to find out more about the Bible? If so what's your next step? Well it's fairly simple really. Pick one up. You can even find the Bible on line these days. I'd recommend you begin with a simple study of the Bible. The following would be good titles to start with:

1. *The Beginning of Everything: A study on Genesis 1-11*
   Every day, in our personal life and the life of the world we can see the impact of what happened in those first few chapters of the Bible. Helpful notes bring the significance of these chapters into focus, and speak clearly to us today.
2. *Understanding the Way of Salvation: God's Perfect Plan*
   Why does the human race need to be saved? From what? Read some typical reactions to these questions from different people, and then discover through the Scriptures what God's answer is.
3. *Jesus – who is he? A study in John's Gospel*
   John's Gospel has brought many thousands of people to a saving knowledge of Christ. It was written 'so that through your faith in him you may have life' (John 20:31).
4. *The only way to be good: A study in Romans*
   How can we possibly be good when nothing less than perfection will do? The book of Romans will give you the answer.

Once you've started to make your way through the Word of God you'll definitely find yourself asking questions. In that case books like the following will be useful accompaniments:

1. *The New Thematic Concordance* by Geoffrey Stonier
   This book lists different Bible topics and where you can find them.
2. *Bible Overview* by Steve Levy and Paul Blackham
   Here you get a brilliant introduction to the Bible that helps you get to grips with God's Word and the structure and meaning of it.
3. *Bible Answers* by Derek Prime
   This book answers questions such as What is Christianity? What is Sin? What is God like? As well as many others.

Are You Familiar with the Bible?

Perhaps these stories have ignited something in you that makes you want to discover the Bible once again? What is your next step? Well it's fairly simple really. Pick one up. You can even find the Bible on line these days. I'd recommend you begin with a simple study of the Bible. The following would be good titles to start with:

1. *Saints in Service: 11 Studies of Bible Characters*
   These are people we can relate to with flaws and strengths.
2. *Walking in Love: A study of John's epistles*
   This study shows us what things we can be certain of – such as the love of God, his redeeming work and that we can know him personally.
3. *Finding Christ in the Old Testament: a study in Pre-existence and Prophecy.* This study helps us to see that God's rescue plan for mankind did not begin in the New Testament but was in the Old Testament too.
4. *Get Ready: A study in 1 & 2 Thessalonians.*
   This study reminds us to persevere through this life and to look forward to Christ's return.

Once you've started to rediscover the Word of God you'll definitely find yourself asking questions. In that case books like the following will be useful accompaniments:

1. *The Authority of the Bible* by Colin Peckham
   This book helps you to refute the accusation that science has proved the Bible to be wrong.
2. *Bible Boot Camp* by Richard Mayhue
   Here you will learn from the examples of key Bible characters – those who failed, those who recovered and those who fought to victory.
3. *The Way of the Righteous in the Muck of Life* by Dale Ralph Davis
   This book shows us that in the opening pages of the Psalms, believers discover foundational truth and delight as children of God.
4. *Effective Christian Living* by Jack Selfridge
   These studies on the Fruit of the Spirit will help you to see if there is spiritual growth in your life and if the Holy Spirit is working through you to further God's wonderful plan.

Christian Focus Publications

publishes books for all ages

Our mission statement –
STAYING FAITHFUL
In dependence upon God we seek to help make his infallible
Word, the Bible, relevant. Our aim is to ensure that the Lord
Jesus Christ is presented as the only hope to obtain forgiveness
of sin, live a useful life and look forward to heaven with Him.

REACHING OUT
Christ's last command requires us to reach out to our world
with his gospel. We seek to help fulfil that by publishing books
that point people towards Jesus and help them develop a
Christ-like maturity. We aim to equip all levels of readers for
life, work, ministry and mission.

Books in our adult range are published in three imprints.
Christian Focus contains popular works including biogra-
phies, commentaries, basic doctrine and Christian living.
Our children's books are also published in this imprint.
Mentor focuses on books written at a level suitable for Bible
College and seminary students, pastors, and other serious
readers. The imprint includes commentaries, doctrinal
studies, examination of current issues and church history.
Christian Heritage contains classic writings from the past.

Christian Focus Publications, Ltd,
Geanies House, Fearn, Ross-shire,
IV20 1TW, Scotland, United Kingdom.
www.christianfocus.com